In loving memory of Basil. You were my soulmate, my biggest supporter, my

champion and my love. You gave me the good life…

Oh the memories...

Photo Credit: Patricia Desiderio

The Not Just A Widow Guidebook

A Widow's Guide To Surviving Her New Reality and Transforming Into Her New Self

written by
PATRICIA M. DESIDERIO &
DOUGLAS O. ROBINSON

Karline,

You've always been a great inspiration for me. It's been a pleasure to know you + work with you all these years.

All the best,

Doug

The Not Just A Widow Guidebook

A Widow's Guide To Surviving Her New Reality and Transforming Into Her New Self

Copyright © 2020 by Patricia Desiderio and Douglas Robinson

Printed in the United States of America

First Edition, 2020

ISBN 978-1-7359348-0-8

This publication contain's the authors' opinions and is designed to provide accurate and authoritative information. It is sold with the understanding that the authors, publisher and Not Just A Widow, LLC are not engaged in rendering legal, accounting, investment planning or other professional advice. The reader should seek the services of a qualified professional for such advice; the authors, publisher and Not Just A Widow, LLC cannot be held responsible for any loss incurred as a result of specific investments or planning decisions made by the reader.

Books are available for bulk purchase at a special discount. Contact Not Just A Widow, LLC directly for details via the company's web site below.

Not Just A Widow, LLC
Bel Air, MD

www.NotJustAWidow.com

Table of Contents

Table of Contents

Patty & Basil's Story

Basil and I met on a stereotypical blind date when we were in our 20s. We grew up a couple of towns from each other in the New York metro area. We were both from Italian families. But as things go when two people meet for the first time, we didn't click - at all. He thought I was a scatter brain who had no idea what I wanted out of life. I thought that he was too conservative and strait laced. Needless to say, we had no interest in pursuing each other after that.

Six months later mutual friends somehow convinced us to give another date a shot. Turns out it was a good idea. Despite that dismal first date, we hit it off the second time around. It went so well, I remember telling a friend, "I am going to marry this guy someday." As it turns out, I did. I married my soulmate right before my 25th birthday.

Those early years were great. Since we didn't have children and Basil travelled quite a bit, I threw myself into supporting him and his career. When he went on business trips all over the world, I joined him. I was the extroverted "ying" to his introverted "yang". We loved every experience that life afforded us and made wonderful memories together.

Unfortunately, the first health problems began when Basil had a heart attack at 40. His health never really got better after that. In his 50's, he developed diabetes and heart disease. In his 60's, he was diagnosed with cancer. I remember it was August 2010 when we found out. And of course chemotherapy and radiation followed as he was trying to survive. I had so much hope.

On February 3, 2011, Basil's defibrillator went off in the middle of the night - not once, but three times. I called 911 and he was taken to the emergency room. That was his last night at home, and for almost three weeks he underwent treatment after treatment.

My brother-in-law came out from California to give me a hand with things. All I remember him saying is: "Prepare yourself – this does not look good". But how do you prepare? YOU CAN'T!

On February 20, with his condition spiraling downward, I gave him permission to die. I went home to try and get some sleep, grab a shower, etc… I'll never forget the call from the doctor who told me that Basil had died. It felt as if my world had been flipped upside down. The grief I felt was immense. Nothing could have prepared me for that moment despite knowing that it was coming.

And so on February 21, 2011, Basil died in the middle of the night at the hospital and my world changed forever.

Foreword

I distinctly remember the first time I met Basil. Patty and I already knew each other through our businesses, but following the stock market drop in 2001/2002, they wanted me to take a look at their investments to get another opinion. We sat down at the kitchen table and Basil pulled out all the binders of statements - he had everything organized. A man after my own heart!

I wish I could say Basil's passing was the first time one of my clients was widowed, but it wasn't. Unfortunately, I have quite a bit of experience with it. Helping a client write a book in the aftermath of her husband's death is also something I'm familiar with. Understanding the unique needs and perspective of widows is something that will be required more and more in the coming decades.

According to the 2010 US Census, 40% of women aged 65 and over were widows. The percentage of older American women who are widows has actually been dropping since 1970, and by 2016, that percentage had fallen to just under 34%. But as the US population gets older and older as the Baby Boomers age, the actual number of widows in the US is rapidly increasing.

As any widow will tell you, you feel like you are in a fog when your husband dies. You feel like you are alone because your husband, your other half, is no longer there. We're here to tell you that you are not alone. The statistics prove it.

When Patty and I sat down to talk about writing this book, we had several goals in mind:

- To tell you that YOU are not alone. Your "widow sisters" are here for you.

- To inform you about the important things that need to be done, what questions need to be asked and where to go for answers.

- To introduce you to the peculiar aspects of widowhood that you will experience. People will say the most insensitive things or won't know what to say. Your social identity will change.

- To prepare you for the transformation that you will go through in the coming years. You can't begin to picture who you will be when you come out the other side of this experience.

Foreword

This isn't just a book about grief, although we talk about the knee-buckling heartache. This isn't just a personal finance book, although we talk about the many things you need to do and consider for your financial security. This isn't just a book with feel-good stories to inspire you, although we include the perspectives of other women who have already walked this path before you - and found their new selves in the process.

This is a guidebook. Conceived by a widow to help guide other widows. Inspired by the wisdom of many widows who have generously shared their experiences with us. There is important information that you can reference, exercises for you to do and places for you to write down notes. Our hope is that you will use it as a resource as you continue with your journey.

Patty and I are genuinely sorry for your loss. We know we can't ease your pain, but we hope we can make the coming months easier.

Doug Robinson

Introduction

Before we start, we'd like to quickly talk about how the book is set up and why. Life is a journey and on this journey the world around us changes and we change in response. People move in and out of our lives…change is constant.

This guidebook is about change - your change. You and your husband were on a journey together and you must go on without him. You will reconfigure yourself and your world, and you will do it in stages. You can't predict where you will be in a year or two - or five.

The death of your husband has turned your life upside down. We have identified five stages that you will go through on your personal journey. We have added a timeline, but it is merely a rough guide. Your journey will progress at your own pace.

Stage 1 - His Death and The Days That Follow

This is the first week or so after your husband's death. It centers around the logistics of planning his funeral, telling his world he has died and those people reacting to and acknowledging his death.

Stage 2 - Living Without Him

After the funeral, everyone goes back to their lives and, while your husband's death impacts them, it isn't close to being the same experience as yours. You are left to process your grief and the loss of your partner by yourself. The reality of it all comes crashing down on you in about the first sixty days.

Stage 3 - The Healing Begins

Over the next few months, you begin to process your grief and adjust to your new reality. Your progress is dependent on your ability to accept your new reality and the ensuing changes. As you focus on healing, your old world may struggle to adjust to your new path. You will likely seek out other women who understand what you are experiencing and with whom you can share your feelings without the filter of having known your husband.

Introduction

Stage 4 - Exploring Your New Identity

As the months turn into years, you will transition out of your old life and explore what makes you happy. It is a new experience where you only have to consider your wants and needs without having to include your husband's. You will make adjustments and try new things until you refine yourself. It's ok to not be sure what you want; you will figure it out in time. Allow yourself to simply enjoy the journey.

Stage 5 - Welcome To The New You

You will look back on your journey and wonder how you got here. You will be surprised by your strength, your accomplishments, how your relationships have changed. You will be amazed that your future looks absolutely nothing like what you could have imagined before your husband died.

The goal of our guidebook is to help you on your journey through all five stages. We'd like to help you manage your grief and heal emotionally. We can't be there with you personally, but we can share stories and resources. We can provide you with questions to ask and tasks to complete to help address your financial security.

No matter where you are on your journey, we'd like to hear from you. Contact us through our website www.notjustawidow.com. Let us know if anything in particular helped you, if we forgot something or if there's a perspective we overlooked. This guidebook is about widows helping widows. Above all, remember that even though your husband's death made you a widow. You are not JUST a widow.

Introduction

Stage Structure

Each stage consists of seven components that are designed to address a different aspect of that stage as you move through it.

- ✓ Introduction - A couple of paragraphs describing the stage.

- ✓ Patty's Sisterly Advice - Patty shares her personal experience and perspective at each stage so you have a point of reference.

- ✓ Terms & Concepts - A glossary defining the technical words you are likely to encounter during each stage.

- ✓ Insights & Experiences - A catalogue of some of the unique aspects of widowhood so you know your experiences are common for widows. We asked some other widows to share their perspective as well.

- ✓ Your Grief Journal - A place to write down your thoughts and feelings.

- ✓ Task List Outline - A list of the tasks we're going to cover in each stage.

- ✓ Task Discussion - We look at each task and provide some guidance to complete it.

We hope this workbook is a valuable resource to you in the months and years ahead as you complete your personal transformation.

STAGE 1 CONTENTS

"Grief never ends...but it changes.

Grief is not a sign of weakness...It is an expression of love."

INTRODUCTION

Even if your husband's death didn't happen suddenly, and you did some planning, the days leading up to and immediately after the funeral or memorial service are usually chaotic. Many people are demanding your attention at a time when you would probably prefer to be alone. You put on the "brave face".

In this section we primarily focus on the funeral. What is the funeral experience like from the perspective of a widow? What do all these terms mean that the funeral director is using? What are the important decisions you need to make about a funeral? How does one actually pay for a funeral?

Remember that during these early days your stress levels are through the roof. Your mind and your body are in survival mode. As a result, you are not thinking clearly and struggle to focus. Let people help, but make sure it's people you trust. You are vulnerable.

Looking back on those first few days, I remember the shock when I got the phone call that Basil had died - even though he was in the hospital and sick. The denial is real.

Basil and I didn't do any formal funeral planning, but we had discussed cremation once he got sick. Because Basil and I moved quite a bit, and I wasn't sure that I would stay in Maryland, I wanted the ability to take him with me.

Basil passed away at 2:30am. The hospital was very business-like when they called to tell me he had passed and to come get his personal belongings in the morning. When I got to the hospital they asked me where I wanted to send the body. Thankfully I knew someone who was a funeral director at a local funeral home. Otherwise, I don't know what I would have done. The funeral home took care of everything. Everyone says to do a bunch of research into funeral homes before you make a choice (and you should do as much as you're able), but you really don't have the luxury of time to do extensive research. It's overwhelming to be thinking about the minutia of comparing funeral home price lists when you're trying to come to grips with the fact that your husband just died.

The funeral itself was a blur. I only remember small snippets. There were so many people; some of whom I hadn't seen in quite a while. I stood by the sign-in book greeting people. I remember what I wore.

As I sat and watched people in a daze, I was so scared as I tried to go over everything in my mind. I started to ask myself:

"What am I going to do now?"

PATTY'S SISTERLY ADVICE

Some thoughts on these early days for you:

➡ You are going to feel numb from the stress and grief. That's normal.

➡ You are going to try and keep yourself busy. Every widow does.

➡ You are going to try and "keep it together" when around other people, but you'll fall apart when you are alone. It's ok; we all did it. Let the tears flow.

➡ Making decisions about your husband's body is a surreal experience. Expect healthcare workers to be businesslike. They see death every day. The folks at the funeral home will seem more compassionate in comparison.

➡ Let the funeral director help you right away. They will know exactly what to do with his body. You have a day or two to figure things out, but that's about it.

➡ Let a dear friend or family member help you get through these days and the funeral.

➡ You will feel a wide range of emotions - denial, fear, anger, gut wrenching grief. Your mood can shift suddenly. You'll feel like you're heading down a river towards roaring rapids in a flimsy boat with no paddle.

Do what you need to do to survive. You'll get through this, but it's a nightmare. There's no other way to describe it.

FUNERAL CEREMONY - A religious or ethnic service commemorating the deceased, with the body present. In the United States, this is most commonly held in a church or synagogue.

MEMORIAL CEREMONY/SERVICE - A ceremony commemorating the deceased when the body isn't present. Often it is held well after death.

FUNERAL SERVICES - These are the services that are traditionally associated with a funeral home, including transporting and caring for the body, embalming or refrigeration, cremation, preparing and filing notices, obtaining authorizations and permits and coordinating with third parties such as the cemetery or a church.

FUNERAL DIRECTOR - An employee of the funeral home who works with the widow or other person to make the funeral arrangements. They often have degrees in mortuary science and, depending on state requirements, are licensed.

VIEWING/VISITATION - This is when the family receives friends and extended family at a predetermined time and place. Often this is held at the funeral home, especially if there is a viewing. However, the body doesn't have to be present. It can be a day or two before the funeral, or even the day of the funeral.

CEMETERY SERVICES - These are the services performed at a cemetery and might include: opening and closing the grave; setting up for a graveside service; setting grave liners, vaults, and markers; maintenance of grounds and facilities.

BURIAL - Most commonly, a burial is when the final resting place of the person's remains is in a grave at a cemetery. Cremated remains can be buried as well. Alternatively, remains can also be "buried" in an above ground crypt or mausoleum.

CREMATION - The use of flame or high heat to reduce the body to ash. Remains are then placed in a box or urn.

DIRECT BURIAL OR CREMATION - This is when there is no funeral ceremony, viewing or visitation (other than a brief family viewing) and the body is buried or cremated very shortly after death.

CEREMONY - Historically, the ceremony is the funeral mass or similar religious ceremony. Each process has its unique aspects. There are also ethnic funeral customs that might be followed. When the deceased wasn't religious and there aren't any particular ethnic customs to follow, a memorial service to remember and reflect on the life of the deceased can be held at a home, restaurant or other gathering place.

EMBALMING - The use of chemicals to preserve the body for viewing.

CASKET/COFFIN - A box or chest large enough to bury remains. Traditionally they are made of finished or unfinished wood, but in modern times they can be made of fiberboard, pressed wood or composite materials.

ANATOMICAL DONATION - This is when the deceased's whole body is donated to medical or scientific research. In contrast, organ donation is often for transplant purposes. Anatomical donation is often pre-arranged and after the study is completed, bodies are usually cremated and delivered to the family.

GRAVE LINER - A cover, usually concrete, that fits over the casket in a grave. Its purpose is to prevent the ground from settling. Although not required by state or local laws, many cemeteries require grave liners.

BURIAL VAULT - A grave liner that completely encloses the casket on all sides.

The days surrounding his death and his funeral will be a blur. There will be moments you can't get out of your head, but mostly you'll struggle to recall any of it. This is common and is due to the incredible amount of stress you are experiencing.

This stage is full of activity. People are demanding your attention to help make decisions about the funeral and such. People want to pay their respects. People want to "see how you are doing". People want to talk about your husband. You may not want to see people or talk to them. Everyone is different. Some people may be comforted by having family and friends near by. Other people just want to be left alone. There is no correct way to feel; do what you feel you need to do.

When it comes to acknowledging death, American culture can be a bit odd. As open as we are as a society, we don't know how to react to and talk about death. Some well wishers will struggle to "say the right thing", which may come out awkward. Others will say nothing at all for fear of saying "the wrong thing". You may be surprised by the thoughtful expression of sympathy from someone you didn't expect to hear from, as well as the complete lack of response from a close friend or family member. Try not to read too much into it.

You will undoubtedly encounter people who want to make your loss about them and their experience. They will start with a comment about how awful your loss is, but then quickly twist it into an opportunity to talk about themselves. Feel free to excuse yourself from those types of conversations as quickly as possible. They are an unnecessary drain on your emotions.

Friends and family members will shower you with meals. It will probably be enough to feed a small army and this at a time when you have no appetite. Say thank you, put it in the freezer, or throw it out if you run out of room. It's ok. Mostly it's an expression from the person that they care for you.

As tempting as it might be to "numb the pain", be careful with alcohol and prescription pain killers. A glass of wine can help with frayed nerves, but pain killers are incredibly addictive and should be avoided (unless you're actually taking them for pain management).

YOUR GRIEF JOURNAL

Experts agree that it can be therapeutic to write your thoughts and/or experiences down on paper. The process of writing is more important than what you actually write down. We have provided space below for you to express yourself however you see fit.

YOUR GRIEF JOURNAL

Below is a list of tasks that we suggest you focus on at this stage of your journey. There will be a thorough explanation of each task in the pages that follow. In the early days you are rightly concerned about your future, but try not to dwell too much on what might happen in six months, a year or beyond. Your focus right now should be on getting through the next week.

✓ Find Your Stage 1 Advocate to help you make decisions about the funeral.

✓ Understand how The Funeral Rule protects you when working with funeral homes and cemeteries.

✓ Confirm whether your husband pre-registered for anatomical donation.

✓ Confirm whether your husband pre-paid for funeral and/or burial services.

✓ Determine whether your husband's funeral requires any special considerations impacting the funeral home you select.

✓ Determine how funeral expenses will be paid and the source of funds.

✓ Decide whether your husband will be cremated or buried in a casket at a cemetery.

✓ Are there any religious funeral ceremonies or rituals that need to be incorporated?

✓ Decide if there will be visitations and a ceremony at the funeral home soon after your husband's death or will a remembrance ceremony be held at a later date.

✓ Decide where your husband's final resting place will be.

✓ Taking into account your needs, select a funeral home.

TASKS

INTRODUCTION TO FUNERAL PLANNING

Most people don't do any funeral planning. They then feel vulnerable and rushed to make a decision in the days just after the death of their loved one. The fact is that you don't have the luxury to take days to do research and soul searching to find the perfect solution. Our advice is don't try to do this on your own. Enlist the help of a family member or friend who can ask questions, voice concerns and be your advocate.

For the vast majority of people in the United States, funeral homes and their funeral directors are an integral part of this funeral process. Their job is to make everything go smoothly regardless of the particulars you've chosen. And like most things in life, it's helpful if you have a sense of what you want - or at least what you DON'T want.

The folks at funeral homes can be an immense help to you. The vast majority are good people who want to help you. But like any profession, there are a few bad apples who will take advantage of your vulnerability for their own profit and push products and services you don't want or need.

It is in your best interest to do as much research as you (and your advocate) can do in the short amount of time available. On the following pages, we outlined the most critical decisions you are likely to face.

TASKS

FIND YOUR STAGE 1 ADVOCATE

In the week after your husband's death there are going to be a lot of critical decisions to be made. Almost all of them deal with the funeral process. Funerals are expensive. You're stressed, probably haven't had a decent night's sleep in a while and are overwhelmed and overloaded. Don't try to do this on your own. It's ok to ask for help. Who do you know who can:

➡ Make phone calls to ask questions and get information?

➡ Keep you company and provide support when meeting with the hospital, hospice, funeral home, church, etc...?

➡ Read through the tasks in this stage, go with you to meet the funeral directors and ask questions?

➡ Answer the phone and respond to texts and emails since you won't feel like talking?

Who is someone that comes to mind that is clearheaded and good at getting things done?

_____

_____

_____

_____

TASKS

UNDERSTANDING FUNERAL HOME SERVICES

Funeral homes provide assistance beyond what most people may think of - often behind the scenes.

➡ Coordinating transportation of the body from the place of death to the funeral home, to and from a house of worship for services, to the cemetery, etc...

➡ Completing certified death certificates by gathering information from health care professionals and providing it to the state

➡ Caring for and preserving the body until final disposition

➡ Providing a convenient location for visitations/viewings/memorial services

➡ Offering advice and counsel on the funeral process

➡ Sale of casket and memorial products

➡ Cremation

Funeral homes usually offer packages that contain the most popular services. The casket is often in addition to the service fee. When comparing prices between two funeral homes, you may find a significant difference in cost for seemingly the same service. This is often due to their overhead charges: how many employees they have, how large the facilities are, where the facilities are located, etc...

You may find that a smaller funeral home offers a lower price since your needs are simple, but if your needs are complex, a larger funeral home may be better equipped to assist you.

UNDERSTANDING YOUR PROTECTIONS UNDER THE FUNERAL RULE

The Funeral Rule is a federal law enacted in 1984 that is enforced by the Federal Trade Commission (FTC). The link below will direct you to the FTC's web site for a complete description of your rights under the Funeral Rule. You have rights. There are protections in place. Do not let anyone pressure you into doing something you do not have to do. If you get push back, attitude or a bad feeling from the person you are speaking with, go elsewhere.

The Funeral Rule in brief:

➡ Funeral directors must provide pricing over the telephone if you ask for it.

➡ If you visit the funeral home, they must give you a General Price List which lists items and services and the associated costs.

➡ Get pricing for caskets and outer burial containers before viewing them. Ask if the lower priced items are on the price list.

➡ No state or local law requires the use of a casket for cremation. If the funeral home offers cremation, they must tell you that alternative containers are available and must make them available.

➡ You can buy caskets and urns from sellers other than the funeral home. The funeral home cannot require you to buy items from them, they cannot refuse to handle a casket or urn you provide and they cannot charge a handling fee.

➡ Embalming is not required for every death. Each state has laws about when embalming or refrigeration is required if the body isn't cremated or buried within a certain time frame. The funeral home may require embalming for a public viewing, but this isn't necessarily a state requirement.

Federal Trade Commission's web site:

https://www.consumer.ftc.gov/articles/0300-ftc-funeral-rule

CONFIRM IF YOUR HUSBAND PRE-REGISTERED FOR ANATOMICAL DONATION

Donating a body to science or a medical program is something that usually requires pre-planning. You can't decide to do it post-mortem. If your husband pre-registered for anatomical donation or with a medical research organization, there should be a record of it.

➡ Did your husband complete a form to pre-register with the local anatomical donation program or another medical research organization?.

    ⦿ If yes, provide the organization's contact information to the nursing home, hospital, or doctor in attendance and they will usually contact the program directly to arrange transport of the body. Otherwise, you, a family member or friend can notify them.

    ⦿ Name of anatomical donation program:

    _____

    ⦿ Phone Number: _____

    ⦿ Who notified the program? _____

    ⦿ When was notification made? _____

Notes: _____

_____

_____

_____

_____

_____

_____

TASKS

CONFIRM IF YOUR HUSBAND PRE-PAID FOR FUNERAL OR BURIAL EXPENSES

If your husband purchased a funeral and/or burial package prior to his death, much of the decision making has already been made.

➡ Did you pre-pay for funeral expenses with a funeral home or crematorium?

- If yes, you should tell the nursing home, hospital or doctor in attendance of this and then notify the funeral home or crematorium. The funeral home or crematorium will coordinate transportation.

- Name of funeral home: _____

- Phone Number: _____

- Do you have a copy of the contract and receipt of payment in case there is any confusion over services to be provided? Y/N

. . . .

Notes: _____

_____

_____

_____

_____

_____

_____

TASKS

DETERMINE IF YOUR HUSBAND'S FUNERAL REQUIRES ANY SPECIAL SERVICES

There are four situations where you should ask the funeral home if they can accommodate your needs prior to making a final selection.

➡ Your husband is to be cremated and you want to be present during the cremation.

➡ You have particular religious or ethnic customs that need to be performed at the funeral home.

➡ You have a very large number of attendees. How many people can the funeral home accommodate?

➡ You want a Green Burial or an eco-friendly service.

We'll discuss each separately on the pages that follow, but if there is a particular request or concern you want to address with a funeral home, you can write it below for reference.

Notes: _____

_____

_____

_____

_____

_____

_____

_____

TASKS

SPECIAL FUNERAL SERVICES

➡ Do you want to be present during the cremation?

◉ Most funeral homes do not perform the cremation on-site, but rather transport the body to a regional crematorium that services multiple funeral homes. If you want to be present during the cremation, the funeral home must operate their own crematorium.

◉ Local funeral homes that provide on-site cremation:

_____

_____

_____

➡ Do you require particular religious or ethnic customs be performed at the funeral home?

◉ If yes, you or your advocate will need to contact funeral homes and make sure they are familiar with and can accommodate these customs.

◉ Local funeral homes that can accommodate your requirements:

_____

_____

_____

TASKS

SPECIAL FUNERAL SERVICES

➡ Will there be a very large number (hundreds) of attendees?

- ◉ Not all funeral homes have a building large enough to accommodate hundreds of attendees. In addition, there may be concerns about traffic, parking, the funeral procession, etc…

- ◉ Confirm with the funeral home if their facilities are large enough.

- ◉ Local funeral homes that can handle a large number of mourners:

_____

_____

_____

➡ Do you want a Green Burial or are eco-friendly services important?

- ◉ A Green Burial has more to do with the cemetery, but you will probably want to make sure the funeral home is familiar with these practices as well.

- ◉ Local funeral homes that provide Green Burial or eco-friendly options:

_____

_____

_____

DETERMINE HOW MUCH MONEY IS AVAILABLE FOR FUNERAL EXPENSES

Before the final selection of funeral services and products is made, it is critical that you consider the cost of services and products and how you will pay for them. While the <u>average</u> funeral costs almost $9,000, the range is very wide: from $2,000 to $15,000 or much more. Adding to the budgeting challenge is that very similar products and services can vary dramatically from one funeral home to the next.

The cost of the funeral home services are largely dependent on the following:

➡ The number of visitations.

⦿ The greater the number of visitations, the higher the cost.

➡ Embalming

⦿ While embalming isn't required by law, your circumstances and the timing may require it.

➡ Transportation

⦿ Transport costs take into account not only the use of the funeral home's vehicles, but also the time of their staff.

➡ Casket

⦿ Casket prices can vary from $1,000 for very simple containers designed exclusively for cremations to thousands of dollars for ornate or unique selections.

TASKS

PAYING FOR A FUNERAL

Funeral homes generally require payment in full at the time the arrangements are made. Since these costs are often significant and you may not have the thousands of dollars needed sitting in your checking account, what is the process for paying the funeral home or cemetery?

➡ Cash or Check

- The simplest method is to write a check, but make sure that you have enough money accessible to pay other final expenses or any other bills that are coming up.

➡ Credit Card

- Since credit cards allow you to pay for expenses now and then pay off the credit card balance later, using a credit card can buy you time before life insurance proceeds are paid or other money is freed up.

- Make sure your credit line is large enough to pay the funeral expenses and leave some room for other needs you may have.

- Don't use a credit card if you'll have no means of paying off the balance.

➡ Assignment of insurance proceeds

- If your husband had an individual life insurance policy (not a group life policy through work), then the funeral home can assign a portion of the death benefit to pay the funeral expenses.

- The funeral home has a form they use and will handle the paperwork.

- While this may be a convenient way to cover the funeral expense when you don't have cash, don't go overboard since those insurance proceeds may be necessary for other expenses that you will incur.

➡ Bridge Loan

- In situations where there aren't any other alternatives, many funeral homes work with banks or other lenders to help you get bridge loans.

- You work directly with the lender regarding qualification and loan terms.

- This should be considered as a last resort and you should have a plan for paying it off before you take out the loan.

TASKS

CASKETS

The choice of casket can be a significant cost in the funeral process. Casket prices can easily exceed $10,000. Casket selection is also where you are perhaps the most vulnerable. You may be tempted, in an effort to honor the memory of your husband, to purchase an unnecessarily expensive casket.

This is why the Federal Trade Commission's Funeral Rule has specific protections in place that you should be aware of.

➡ Where can you buy a casket?

- ◉ A funeral home

- ◉ Most cemeteries

- ◉ Large retailers like Walmart, Costco and Sam's Club

- ◉ Online retailers like Casketsite.com and Overnightcaskets.com

➡ What are the rules if I purchase a casket from a funeral home or cemetery?

- ◉ The Funeral Rules apply and the funeral home or cemetery must provide a price list of available caskets prior to showing you the caskets.

➡ What are the rules if I purchase a casket from a retailer?

- ◉ The Funeral Rule doesn't require the retailer to provide a casket price list.

- ◉ The funeral home has to accept the casket from the retailer and they cannot charge a handling fee.

TASKS

WAYS TO REDUCE CASKET COSTS

Buying a casket from a funeral home is the most convenient thing to do when you are overwhelmed by decisions and you are trying to get things done quickly. It is possible, with minimal effort, to reduce casket costs:

➡ Buy from a third-party retailer.

➡ Alternative Container - For cremation, there is the Alternative Container option, which is a very inexpensive fiberboard or composite container. They generally cost less than $500.

➡ Casket rental - if your husband is to be cremated, and you choose a very inexpensive cremation casket or alternative container, some funeral homes can rent you a nicer looking casket more suitable for visitations and the funeral.

TASKS

ARE THERE RELIGIOUS CEREMONIES OR RITUALS?

If there will be a religious ceremony at a church, synagogue or other house of worship, the funeral home needs to know about it.

➡ Does the body need to be transported to and from the house of worship?

➡ Will there be pallbearers or will the casket need to be moved during the ceremony?

　　⦿ Who will assist with moving the casket?

_____

_____

_____

➡ Name of the house of worship or location of ceremony:

_____

_____

_____

➡ Contact person's name and phone/email:

_____

_____

_____

TASKS

WILL THERE BE VISITATIONS AND/OR A MEMORIAL CEREMONY?

In modern times, you have numerous options regarding a funeral ceremony. A traditional funeral service involves a visitation at the funeral home, ceremony at a house of worship and a burial at the cemetery soon after death. As families have spread out and religious practices change, many Americans are opting for different and more customized funeral services. Regardless of the services you choose, experts agree that it is a critical part of the grieving process that there be some sort of ceremony acknowledging the death of a loved one. Here are some of the things you might consider if you decide a "traditional" funeral isn't the best path for you and your family.

Visitation

These are typically held at the funeral home in the days immediately following death. Pictures and/or videos of your husband can be displayed. The body can be present or not. It can be open casket or not. The purpose of the visitation is to give your husband's family, friends, colleagues, etc… an opportunity to "pay their respects" and acknowledge the death of a person who was an important part of their life. You can have a visitation even if your husband is to be cremated.

Memorial Ceremony

Not everyone wants a religious ceremony. A memorial ceremony is a formal opportunity for family and friends to acknowledge the death of your husband. Funeral homes can provide a location for the ceremony and can help coordinate the ceremony. If you need someone to give a eulogy, there are people who are trained to do this. The ceremony can be weeks or months after the death depending on the need to coordinate with attendees or other circumstances. Generally, it is advisable to hold the ceremony as soon as possible to aid in the grieving process.

TASKS

WHERE WILL YOUR HUSBAND'S FINAL RESTING PLACE BE?

There are two questions to answer regarding your husband's final disposition: where and when? Perhaps your husband will be buried at the church's cemetery right after the funeral ceremony. Perhaps you want to keep your husband's ashes with you after he is cremated. There is no correct answer. Do what feels right. However, you'll need to give some direction to the funeral home so they can assist you. Your options hinge on whether or not your husband is to be cremated.

➡ If he will be buried in a cemetery:

- ◉ The burial will need to be soon after death unless embalming is performed.

- ◉ Embalming allows the burial to occur up to several months after death.

- ◉ What cemetery will he be buried at?

- ◉ Do you already own a plot?

➡ If he will be cremated:

- ◉ Interment of ashes is the practice of burying the remains in a permanent place.

- ◉ The interment can be at a time of your choosing. Soon after his death or months or even years later.

- ◉ Is there a specific location where the remains are to be interred - church, cemetery, memorial garden? Is it local or is travel required?

- ◉ Are his ashes to be disbursed or spread at a location that was meaningful to him? Where is the location and when will the disbursement occur?

Notes: _____

_____

_____

_____

_____

_____

_____

STAGE 2 CONTENTS

"The Only Cure For Grief Is Grieving"

INTRODUCTION

During the days after your husband's death, you're usually so busy with planning the funeral and dealing with the constant stream of friends and family that you struggle to stay afloat. Everything is a blur. But almost every widow will tell you that the days AFTER the funeral is when reality comes crashing down. We define Stage 2 as the sixty days after your husband's death. Often described as The Fog, it is when family and friends go back to their lives and you are left to figure out how in the world you're going to survive.

In this section of the guidebook, we're going to talk about what you're experiencing emotionally, some coping mechanisms, and how to get help. We're going to discuss administrative and financial tasks you need to address - and the ones you should put off until later.

These early days are completely horrible. It will get better. But in this section we're just trying to help you keep your head above water.

PATTY'S SISTERLY ADVICE

Basil's funeral was a week after he died. My brother-in-law Carmen, who was here for three weeks, returned to California. My sister came to the funeral and stayed a few days. She had to return to New York for work. Local friends and family all went back to their lives and routines.

For the first time in thirty-four years, I was alone. This was my reality. The sense of loss was…indescribable. I was numb. But you know that.

I could barely eat. Sleep escaped me. I lost track of the days. The first two months were just a blur. The grief was overwhelming, and I felt like I was in a fog.

We never had children and my business was home based, so the silence was deafening.

I was hurting and I so desperately needed my Basil. I took for granted how much his mere presence meant to me. I kept waiting for him to walk through the front door. But of course he didn't.

If someone asked me what I did for the two months after Basil died, I'd say I mostly stared off into nothing and cried. Looking back on that time, it's easy to ask: "How could you do nothing for two months?" But if you're in the middle of it, you know what I'm talking about.

I still distinctly remember that week after Basil's memorial service and the overwhelming sense of loss. All around the house are letters and cards and flowers, but the thoughts and prayers don't come close to filling the void.

➡ You are going to feel alone. So alone.

➡ You won't feel like doing anything and may find yourself staring into space. We've all done that.

➡ You may not feel like talking to anyone, answering the phone or emails. It's just another reminder that he's gone. You toy with not answering communications. You pretend to not be home.

You won't feel like eating – or maybe you binge eat. Your whole world has changed. Now is the time to make sure you eat healthy and sleep.

You need to take care of yourself and your heart. Stress - especially prolonged stress like you are experiencing right now - does awful things to your body. It can send you to the hospital or kill you.

You don't want to get sick. All I kept asking myself was "What happens if I get sick?" Who will take care of me?

I know it will be hard, but try not to isolate yourself from others. Force yourself to answer that letter, that phone call, that e-mail. You will feel better for it!

If you feel like talking, call someone who is a good listener. If you want company, but don't want to talk, find someone who can just be there without constant chatter.

Don't worry about the future, just get through the day...

GRIEF - Deep sorrow; sadness; distress.

PROLONGED/COMPLICATED GRIEF DISORDER - Everyone experiences grief in their own personal way. Normally, the grief fades over time. Again, this time period will vary. But it is estimated that nearly 10% of all bereaved develop prolonged grief and women are more susceptible than men. If the pain of your loss doesn't seem to have lessened six months after your husband's death, you should seek help.

EMOTIONAL SYMPTOMS OF GRIEF

➡ Inability to show or experience joy

➡ Bitterness

➡ Numbness or Detachment

➡ Preoccupation with loss

➡ Digestive problems

➡ Fatigue

➡ Headaches and Chest Pain

➡ Sore muscles

PHYSICAL SYMPTOMS OF GRIEF

Source: https://www.psychguides.com/grief-management/

CERTIFIED DEATH CERTIFICATE - The official document issued by the state where a person's death occurs. Usually the division of vital records produces the form. It contains important information about your husband and has a raised seal. Many institutions require it as proof of death.

GROUP LIFE INSURANCE - Larger employers often provide basic life insurance to their employees for little to no cost. The standard death benefit is equivalent to the employee's base salary. The employee usually has the option to purchase additional insurance as well.

COBRA - The acronym for the bill that gave workers and their families the right to continue group health benefits. COBRA allows workers in most situations to continue health coverage for eighteen (18) months. In the case of the death of a worker, the covered spouse and children can extend coverage for up thirty-six (36) months.

RETIREMENT PLAN - There are a number of different types of retirement plans employers offer employees. The most common are 401(k)s and 403(b)s. There are also pension plans, SEPs, and SIMPLEs. Federal employees have access to the Thrift Savings Plan (TSP).

PENSION - A pension is monthly payments from a former employer. When the pension owner dies, the payments may stay the same, get reduced or stop altogether depending on the payout selected when the pension was started.

ANNUITY - An annuity is an insurance product. Annuities are very complex and there are many options available.

LIFE INSURANCE TERMS

OWNER - The person or entity who legally owns the policy and therefore has the authority to make changes to the policy. For example, changing the address or beneficiary. The owner is also responsible for paying the premiums. The owner can be changed.

INSURED - The person whose death it is insured against. The insured doesn't have to be the owner. When the insured dies, the death benefit is paid. The insured can not be changed.

BENEFICIARY - The person, people or entity (i.e. a trust or estate) named in the policy to receive the death benefit. If no one is named, the proceeds are most often paid to the insured's estate since the owner and insured are often the same.

CONTRACT/POLICY NUMBER - The number or combination of numbers and letters that uniquely identifies the policy.

PREMIUM - The amount that needs to be paid to keep the policy in force.

DEATH BENEFIT - The amount of money beneficiaries will receive upon the death of the insured.

CASH SURRENDER VALUE - The amount of money the owner will receive if the life insurance policy is surrendered or terminated.

INSURER - The insurance company that insures the life of the insured.

INSURANCE AGENT - The salesperson who sold the policy and/or is responsible for servicing the policy by being a point of contact between the insurance company and policy owner.

DID YOU KNOW?

➡ 800,000 people are widowed each year and 700,000 of those people are women.

➡ Most widows live in poverty – over 115 million worldwide.

➡ "Death of a spouse" is listed as the #1 stressor on the stress index and is considered one of life's most devastating events.

➡ 60% of those who lose a spouse or significant other will experience a serious illness within 12 months.

➡ Insomnia is one of the most common symptoms for a grieving spouse.

➡ The average age of widowhood is 55.

➡ Most widows lose 75% of their support base when their spouse dies.

➡ Scamming and manipulation from others are commonly perpetrated toward widows.

➡ Most widows lose touch with their in-laws within a year of a loss.

➡ Is it really possible to die of a broken heart? Yes, widows have a 30% elevated risk of death in the first 6 months after their spouse dies.

➡ Almost half of women over 65 years of age in the US are widows and about seven out of ten of these women live alone.

These are the statistics, but let's talk about the real world …. OH, WAIT, this is the real world!

THE WIDOW FOG / WIDOW BRAIN

You will likely experience a phenomenon called "Widow Fog" or "Widow Brain". It is a real thing that affects all people who experience such a traumatic loss. It beats you down and leaves you helpless and confused during a time when there is very little room for such things.

It is caused by your brain trying to protect you from the pain. It begins at the loss and can vary in duration and intensity among individuals. It is often described as feeling disconnected, on autopilot, or in a state of mindless motion.

You have many thoughts but lack the ability to organize and focus. The ability to recall, reason and plan seems overwhelming. You may have memory gaps - like amnesia. You remember point A to B but point B to C is fleeting. Your brain is in overload. This is very common in the beginning and people who are grieving go through this.

The first thing you need to know is that this experience is universal and normal. Don't panic that something is wrong with you. Second, you need to realize that you will function again. Your focus and awareness will return over time.

THE WIDOW FOG / WIDOW BRAIN (continued)

There is science behind the Widow Fog. There is a part of your brain called the Pre-Frontal Cortex (PFC) that assists in rational thinking and making sense of your emotions. It is connected to every other part of your brain and operates as your command center. The main functions of the PFC are to:

➡ Understand and Decide

➡ Recall and Memorize

➡ Inhibit

Your PFC can only process one thing at a time. So the PFC is very limited in its capacity to hold information.

Widow Fog / Widow Brain is the manifestation of your PFC run amok. Your PFC is perpetually overloaded by trying to hold and process too much information under conditions of utter depletion. The overload of information rapidly exhausts your PFC, and your exhausted PFC fails you in its job of thinking rationally and making sense of emotion.

Your grief involves being perpetually caught off guard by the type and magnitude of emotions. You find yourself trying your hardest to make sense of it through rational thinking—the stories you tell yourself to explain things. Just when you think things are settled, a tornado of thoughts and feelings tosses everything back up in the air for you to begin sorting again. All the while, you are on autopilot, only able to perform the most routine tasks—if you even remember to do them. As mentioned in this workbook, there are plenty of things to get done when your husband passes. Things that need to be done immediately. That is why finding that advocate (as referenced in Stage 1) is so important!

Be prepared for people to say insensitive, offensive, or just plain stupid things to you at a time when your emotions are raw and you patience is short.

"It's a good thing you travelled when you did."

Be prepared for seemingly innocuous comments to grate on your nerves. Comments that before your husband's death you wouldn't have thought twice about.

"You're a strong woman. You'll get through this."

Very quickly, you're going to find yourself dealing with things you relied on your husband to take care of in the past. For example, car maintenance and dealing with the mechanic, house repairs and dealing with the handyman.

"It was a hot summer day and storms started rolling in - wind and rain, branches hitting the house. The electricity goes out. I drag the generator from the shed. There's no gas. I grab the empty gas can and drive around to find an open gas station. I get home with the gas and realize I don't know how to work this thing. I sat for a while feeling sorry for myself. I wanted to do it myself, but had to call a neighbor over to help me. I was just so overwhelmed; crying, wishing my husband was there to help."

Relief. It's an emotion that widows sometimes carry with them as a deep, dark secret. If your husband suffered a long illness before he died, it's natural to feel relief from the stress and anxiety of carrying the burden with him and taking care of him. Feeling relief doesn't mean you're happy he died.

Sainting of the spouse occurs when a widow puts her husband on a pedestal. Not all marriages are fairy tales; not all husbands are kind and caring. If your husband's death released you from a troubled marriage, don't feel guilty for feeling a sense of freedom. Don't compensate for that guilt by painting an inaccurate picture of your husband's character.

YOUR GRIEF JOURNAL

Experts agree that it can be therapeutic to write your thoughts and/or experiences down on paper. The process of writing is more important than what you actually write down. We have provided space below for you to express yourself however you see fit.

YOUR GRIEF JOURNAL

In the two months after your husband's death, the tasks you should focus on include some important notifications and gathering important documents and information that will be needed in Stage 3 and beyond. Below is a list of tasks that we suggest you focus on at this stage of your journey. We explain each task in the pages that follow. Focus only on what needs to get done in the next several weeks. We've put the tasks you should work on first at the top of the list.

✓ Find your Stage 2 advocate.

✓ Obtain certified death certificates.

✓ Notify employer and investigate employee benefits.

✓ Locate important papers/documents.

✓ Notify Social Security.

✓ Make a list of sources of income and major expenses.

✓ Notify the income payers.

✓ Pay bills.

✓ Claim Life Insurance.

✓ Make a list of important web sites and your husband's log in information.

TASK OUTLINE

It's natural in the early days to feel overwhelmed. This is partly due to the uncertainty of the future, but it's also because you know that there are all these things that need to be done. Focus on the tasks we present in each stage and you'll be fine. Just as importantly, below is a list of things <u>you do not need to do right now</u>.

🚫 Register your husband's Will or distribute assets or property

🚫 Sell your house

🚫 Buy life insurance

🚫 Buy a car

🚫 Buy or sell investments (mutual funds, stocks, bonds)

🚫 Withdraw money from your IRA or retirement plan

🚫 Redecorate

🚫 Go on an expensive vacation

🚫 Give away money to family, friends, charities or religious groups

🚫 Borrow money

🚫 Anything that can't be easily reversed

🚫 Plan the rest of your life...

TASKS

FIND YOUR STAGE 2 ADVOCATE

Hopefully you had a close friend or family member to help through the first stage. They likely needed to go back to their life after the funeral. Make sure you tell them how much you appreciated their help.

In Stage 2, grief sets in, you have the chance to think about what's happened and the uncertainty of the future overwhelms you. Don't try to do too much. We've outlined the most critical tasks to consider completing at this stage and if you can find someone to help you get them done, you'll be much better off. Who do you know that can help you:

➡ Complete the tasks in Stage 2.

➡ Do some research on the internet or make some phone calls for you.

➡ Attend meetings with you to ask questions and take notes.

➡ Who comes to mind that is clearheaded and good at getting things done?

Notes: _____

_____

_____

_____

_____

_____

_____

OBTAIN CERTIFIED DEATH CERTIFICATES

In most cases the funeral home is the one who handles filing the necessary official paperwork with the state. It can take several days to process this paperwork and get an official certified death certificate. On the next page we provide an example of what a certified death certificate looks like.

Typical components include:

➡ Printed on legal sized (8.5" x 14") paper

➡ Have the words "Certification" or "Certificate of Vital Record" at the top

➡ Have a raised seal (stamp) from the Department of Health

➡ Have a certificate number (often in red ink)

➡ List the decedent's information and the cause of death

The funeral home will likely give you a free death certificate or two, but that isn't enough.

As soon as the certified death certificate is available, tell the funeral home that you want to order another ten (10) copies in addition to what they have given you. There will likely be a small cost, but it is worth it.

Of the companies to whom you will present the death certificate, some may scan the certificate or make a photo copy and return the original to you. Others will insist they need to keep an official copy.

EXAMPLE OF A CERTIFIED DEATH CERTIFICATE

U.S. STANDARD CERTIFICATE OF DEATH

LOCAL FILE NO.   STATE FILE NO.

1. DECEDENT'S LEGAL NAME (Include AKA's if any) (First, Middle, Last)	2. SEX	3. SOCIAL SECURITY NUMBER

4a. AGE-Last Birthday (Years)	4b. UNDER 1 YEAR		4c. UNDER 1 DAY		5. DATE OF BIRTH (Mo/Day/Yr)	6. BIRTHPLACE (City and State or Foreign Country)
	Months	Days	Hours	Minutes		

7a. RESIDENCE-STATE   7b. COUNTY   7c. CITY OR TOWN

7d. STREET AND NUMBER   7e. APT. NO.   7f. ZIP CODE   7g. INSIDE CITY LIMITS? ☐ Yes ☐ No

8. EVER IN US ARMED FORCES? ☐ Yes ☐ No	9. MARITAL STATUS AT TIME OF DEATH ☐ Married ☐ Married, but separated ☐ Widowed ☐ Divorced ☐ Never Married ☐ Unknown	10. SURVIVING SPOUSE'S NAME. (If wife, give name prior to first marriage)

11. FATHER'S NAME (First, Middle, Last)   12. MOTHER'S NAME PRIOR TO FIRST MARRIAGE (First, Middle, Last)

13a. INFORMANT'S NAME	13b. RELATIONSHIP TO DECEDENT	13c. MAILING ADDRESS (Street and Number, City, State, Zip Code)

14. PLACE OF DEATH (Check only one: see instructions)

IF DEATH OCCURRED IN A HOSPITAL:
☐ Inpatient ☐ Emergency Room/Outpatient ☐ Dead on Arrival

IF DEATH OCCURRED SOMEWHERE OTHER THAN A HOSPITAL:
☐ Hospice facility ☐ Nursing home/Long term care facility ☐ Decedent's home ☐ Other (Specify):

15. FACILITY NAME (If not institution, give street & number)	16. CITY OR TOWN , STATE, AND ZIP CODE	17. COUNTY OF DEATH

18. METHOD OF DISPOSITION: ☐ Burial ☐ Cremation ☐ Donation ☐ Entombment ☐ Removal from State ☐ Other (Specify)	19. PLACE OF DISPOSITION (Name of cemetery, crematory, other place)

20. LOCATION-CITY, TOWN, AND STATE	21. NAME AND COMPLETE ADDRESS OF FUNERAL FACILITY

22. SIGNATURE OF FUNERAL SERVICE LICENSEE OR OTHER AGENT	23. LICENSE NUMBER (Of Licensee)

ITEMS 24-28 MUST BE COMPLETED BY PERSON WHO PRONOUNCES OR CERTIFIES DEATH	24. DATE PRONOUNCED DEAD (Mo/Day/Yr)	25. TIME PRONOUNCED DEAD
26. SIGNATURE OF PERSON PRONOUNCING DEATH (Only when applicable)	27. LICENSE NUMBER	28. DATE SIGNED (Mo/Day/Yr)

29. ACTUAL OR PRESUMED DATE OF DEATH (Mo/Day/Yr) (Spell Month)	30. ACTUAL OR PRESUMED TIME OF DEATH	31. WAS MEDICAL EXAMINER OR CORONER CONTACTED? ☐ Yes ☐ No

CAUSE OF DEATH (See instructions and examples)

32. PART I. Enter the chain of events--diseases, injuries, or complications--that directly caused the death. DO NOT enter terminal events such as cardiac arrest, respiratory arrest, or ventricular fibrillation without showing the etiology. DO NOT ABBREVIATE. Enter only one cause on a line. Add additional lines if necessary.

Approximate interval: Onset to death

IMMEDIATE CAUSE (Final disease or condition ------> resulting in death)   a._____
Due to (or as a consequence of):

Sequentially list conditions, if any, leading to the cause listed on line a. Enter the UNDERLYING CAUSE (disease or injury that initiated the events resulting in death) LAST   b._____
Due to (or as a consequence of):

c._____
Due to (or as a consequence of):

d._____

PART II. Enter other significant conditions contributing to death but not resulting in the underlying cause given in PART I	33. WAS AN AUTOPSY PERFORMED? ☐ Yes ☐ No
	34. WERE AUTOPSY FINDINGS AVAILABLE TO COMPLETE THE CAUSE OF DEATH? ☐ Yes ☐ No

35. DID TOBACCO USE CONTRIBUTE TO DEATH? ☐ Yes ☐ Probably ☐ No ☐ Unknown	36. IF FEMALE: ☐ Not pregnant within past year ☐ Pregnant at time of death ☐ Not pregnant, but pregnant within 42 days of death ☐ Not pregnant, but pregnant 43 days to 1 year before death ☐ Unknown if pregnant within the past year	37. MANNER OF DEATH ☐ Natural ☐ Homicide ☐ Accident ☐ Pending Investigation ☐ Suicide ☐ Could not be determined

38. DATE OF INJURY (Mo/Day/Yr) (Spell Month)	39. TIME OF INJURY	40. PLACE OF INJURY (e.g., Decedent's home; construction site; restaurant; wooded area)	41. INJURY AT WORK? ☐ Yes ☐ No

42. LOCATION OF INJURY: State: City or Town:

Street & Number: Apartment No.:   Zip Code:

43. DESCRIBE HOW INJURY OCCURRED:	44. IF TRANSPORTATION INJURY, SPECIFY: ☐ Driver/Operator ☐ Passenger ☐ Pedestrian ☐ Other (Specify)

45. CERTIFIER (Check only one):
☐ Certifying physician-To the best of my knowledge, death occurred due to the cause(s) and manner stated.
☐ Pronouncing & Certifying physician-To the best of my knowledge, death occurred at the time, date, and place, and due to the cause(s) and manner stated.
☐ Medical Examiner/Coroner-On the basis of examination, and/or investigation, in my opinion, death occurred at the time, date, and place, and due to the cause(s) and manner stated.

Signature of certifier:_____

46. NAME, ADDRESS, AND ZIP CODE OF PERSON COMPLETING CAUSE OF DEATH (Item 32)

47. TITLE OF CERTIFIER	48. LICENSE NUMBER	49. DATE CERTIFIED (Mo/Day/Yr)	50. FOR REGISTRAR ONLY- DATE FILED (Mo/Day/Yr)

51. DECEDENT'S EDUCATION-Check the box that best describes the highest degree or level of school completed at the time of death.	52. DECEDENT OF HISPANIC ORIGIN? Check the box that best describes whether the decedent is Spanish/Hispanic/Latino. Check the "No" box if decedent is not Spanish/Hispanic/Latino.	53. DECEDENT'S RACE (Check one or more races to indicate what the decedent considered himself or herself to be)
☐ 8th grade or less		☐ White
☐ 9th - 12th grade; no diploma		☐ Black or African American
☐ High school graduate or GED completed	☐ No, not Spanish/Hispanic/Latino	☐ American Indian or Alaska Native (Name of the enrolled or principal tribe)_____
☐ Some college credit, but no degree	☐ Yes, Mexican, Mexican American, Chicano	☐ Asian Indian ☐ Chinese
☐ Associate degree (e.g., AA, AS)	☐ Yes, Puerto Rican	☐ Filipino ☐ Japanese
☐ Bachelor's degree (e.g., BA, AB, BS)	☐ Yes, Cuban	☐ Korean ☐ Vietnamese
☐ Master's degree (e.g., MA, MS, MEng, MEd, MSW, MBA)	☐ Yes, other Spanish/Hispanic/Latino (Specify)_____	☐ Other Asian (Specify)_____ ☐ Native Hawaiian
☐ Doctorate (e.g., PhD, EdD) or Professional degree (e.g., MD, DDS, DVM, LLB, JD)		☐ Guamanian or Chamorro ☐ Samoan ☐ Other Pacific Islander (Specify)_____ ☐ Other (Specify)_____

54. DECEDENT'S USUAL OCCUPATION (Indicate type of work done during most of working life. DO NOT USE RETIRED):

55. KIND OF BUSINESS/INDUSTRY

REV. 11/2003

Courtesy of the US Centers for Disease Control and Prevention

USING CERTIFIED DEATH CERTIFICATES

You will need certified death certificates to:

➡ Change the registration of bank accounts

➡ Cancel or change cell phone service

➡ Remove your husband's name from the utility bills

➡ Transfer ownership of or sell an automobile

➡ Update home and auto insurance policies

➡ Notify IRA and retirement plan custodians

➡ Notify the mortgage company

➡ Remove your husband from your home's deed

➡ Sell your home

Protect yourself! The death certificate has all of your husband's personal information on it: date of birth, Social Security number, etc... Identity thieves will use this information.

Keep a copy or two in a safe place (such as a fire proof filing cabinet). It's not uncommon to need a copy of the death certificate years later to accomplish some piece of legal or financial business.

TASKS

NOTIFY EMPLOYER & INVESTIGATE EMPLOYEE BENEFITS

If your husband was employed at his death, his colleagues are no doubt aware of his death. You will need to officially notify his employer. Ask his direct supervisor who to contact.

Employer Contact Name: _____

Employer Contact Phone: _____

Employer Contact Email: _____

Here are some additional things to ask about:

➡ Last paycheck

  ◉ When will it be paid? _____

  ◉ Did your husband have accrued sick or vacation days that will be paid out?

➡ Employer group life insurance

  ◉ Many employers offer group life insurance to their employees for little or no cost to the employee. Ask the benefits contact at the employer if your husband has any group life insurance. If yes, ask who to contact to put in the claim.

  ◉ Group Life Insurance? YES / NO

  ◉ Group Life Insurance Company: _____

  ◉ Group Life Insurance Phone: _____

  ◉ Group Life Web Site: _____

  ◉ Group Life Insurance Death Benefit: _____

➡ Health Insurance

  ◉ Did you have health insurance through your husband's employer? YES / NO

  ◉ If yes, you are eligible to continue coverage under COBRA. We discuss health insurance more in Stage 3, but for right now the easiest thing to do is just keep that coverage in force until things settle down. The benefits person at your husband's employer will send you information about COBRA and how to make premium payments.

DOCUMENT EMPLOYER RETIREMENT PLAN INFORMATION

If your husband was employed at his death, there is a good chance he participated in a retirement plan sponsored by his employer. He may or may not have been actively contributing to the plan at the time of his death. Even if he wasn't, he might have an open account.

There are a number of different types of plans, an employer can have multiple plans, and the terminology and rules can be very confusing. Your best place to start to get information is the human resources (HR) contact.

Ask the HR contact about the current retirement plan(s) and if your husband had a balance in the plan(s).

Name of retirement plan: _____

Type of retirement plan: _____

Sponsor or custodian of plan: _____

Phone number or web site where you can get current information: _____

Ask if there are other current retirement plans, terminated plans or frozen plans?

YES/NO

If YES, document the same information about the plan as the current plan.

Right now, don't do anything with the plan. Don't do a distribution, withdrawal or rollover. Leave it alone unless the account balance is under $5,000 and the employer notifies you that they are processing a mandatory cash out or rollover. If that happens, talk to a financial planner immediately for advice.

As the spouse of a deceased employee, there are special rules that apply to you. You will have some choices to make, but it is too early to make those decisions. We'll address the topic later.

TASKS

LOCATE IMPORTANT PAPERS/DOCUMENTS

In the coming weeks and months, there will be many legal and financial tasks you will need to complete. You may be asked for certain legal documents and other important papers, so it's best to start getting them together now. While you're waiting for the death certificate, gather these documents/items:

➡ Birth Certificate

⦿ Birth certificates can be a source of frustration in today's world. You may have a birth notice from the hospital, baptismal certificate or some other official looking birth record, but they aren't official state issued birth certificates. If you find you need to get one, most states' division of vital records allow you to order them on their web site for a nominal fee. Just type "Maryland birth certificate" (for example) into your web browser. Make sure you go to the state's official web site.

➡ Marriage Certificate

➡ Driver's License

➡ Military Discharge papers

➡ Will (alternatively may be called a Simple Will or Last Will and Testament)

➡ Living Trust (alternatively called a Revocable Trust) and/or any other Trust papers

➡ Social Security card

➡ Life Insurance policy(ies)

➡ Vehicle Title and registration

➡ Credit cards

TASKS

Social Security Administration Benefits

The Social Security Administration (SSA) is usually notified of your husband's death by the funeral home in the process of completing the paperwork for the death certificate. Even if your husband wasn't currently receiving benefits, you should call the SSA or visit your local Social Security office.

Social Security Administration's web site: www.SSA.gov

Social Security Administration's Phone: 1-800-772-1213

Here are some additional things to be aware of:

➡ Special Lump-Sum Death Payment - $255 is paid to the surviving spouse or child if they meet certain requirements.

➡ If your husband was receiving benefits, you must return the benefit for the month of death and any later months. If benefits were being direct deposited, the SSA will "pull back" any benefits that need to be returned. If paid by check, do not deposit those checks.

➡ Survivor benefits widows may receive:

  ◉ Monthly payments if you are at least age 60.

  ◉ Monthly payments if you are disabled and at least age 50.

  ◉ Monthly payments if you are caring for a child under the age of 16.

➡ Survivor benefits your children may receive

  ◉ Monthly payments if they are under the age of 18 or disabled.

➡ A person can only receive one benefit at a time.

  ◉ If you were both retired and receiving benefits when he died, you will only receive one of those benefits going forward. It will be the higher of the two monthly benefits.

TASKS

CONTACTING THE SOCIAL SECURITY ADMINISTRATION

We strongly suggest that you go to your local Social Security office and speak to them about your survivor benefits as soon as possible. They have all your husband's information on file and can provide further guidance. You can call the SSA's general phone number to make an appointment at your local office.

1-800-772-1213

Local Social Security Administration office address:

_____

_____

_____

_____

Appointment Date: _____

TASKS

DOCUMENT SOURCES OF INCOME AND MAJOR EXPENSES

In the coming weeks, you'll need to make notifications. We'll cover these in the next several tasks. But now is a good time to begin reviewing and monitoring bank and credit card statements and transactions.

➡ Review bank account transactions for deposits. Make a list of all payers and the amounts. For now, just make the list. Later we'll help you start the notification process.

   ⊙ Common sources of income are employer salary, Social Security benefits, retiree pension payments, annuity payments and distributions from investment accounts or IRAs.

➡ Review bank account and credit card statements for major routine expenses. Make a list of the company, the amount, the date, and whether it is an individual or joint expense. For now, just make the list. Later we'll help you start the notification process..

   ⊙ Common expenses are mortgage payments, rent payments, car (or other vehicle) payments, insurance premiums, utilities, mobile phone plans, TV and streaming service subscriptions, condo or homeowners' association fees.

➡ Review your most recent income tax return for any sources of income you missed. If you can't find the return or don't know where to look, call the person/company that completed the return (if you know who that is). If your husband used tax software to complete the return, you may need to ask someone for help getting the information.

TASKS

DOCUMENT SOURCES OF INCOME AND MAJOR EXPENSES

Income or Expense Description	Amount	Most Recent Transaction Date

TASKS

NOTIFY INCOME PAYERS

Depending on the list you created previously, there may be nothing to do here. If your husband died prior to his retirement and he was working, you should have already notified his employer. Likewise, Social Security has already been notified and hopefully you've talked to them or have an appointment scheduled to learn about your survivor benefits. This is especially important if you have minor children.

Now is the time to notify any other entities that were paying your husband income. Here's the process you can follow for each one.

➡ Start with a phone call. Call the company using the number on the statement or try their web site.

➡ Tell them who you are and that your husband has passed.

➡ Ask them what their process is to officially update their records.

  ◉ Do they need an original death certificate or is a copy acceptable?

  ◉ Are there forms you need to complete? How do you get them? Where do you return them?

  ◉ Does the last payment need to be returned?

➡ Ask them if there are any survivor benefits.

  ◉ Can they tell you what they are over the phone?

  ◉ Will you receive them automatically or do you have to complete a form?

On the next two pages we've provided worksheets to gather this information. If you need additional worksheets, you can download them from our web site at **www.notjustawidow.com**.

Income Payer Notification Worksheet

Instructions: Use this worksheet to keep track of the income payers - who they are; when you notified them; who you spoke to; when you sent them forms. (You can download a digital pdf copy of this worksheet at www.notjustawidow.com/worksheets)

Income Payer Name:

Account/Reference Number:

Phone Number: Date Called/Notified:

Representative's Name:

Is original death certificate required? _____ YES / NO

Is there a survivor benefit? _____ YES / NO

Do forms need to be completed? _____ YES / NO

Where can you get the forms?

Date forms received/downloaded?

Where to send: Date sent:

Method: Mail / Overnight / Email / Fax

Additional Notes:

Income Payer Notification Worksheet

Income Payer Name:

Account/Reference Number:

Phone Number: Date Called/Notified:

Representative's Name:

Is original death certificate required? _____ YES / NO

Is there a survivor benefit? _____ YES / NO

Do forms need to be completed? _____ YES / NO

Where can you get the forms?

Date forms received/downloaded?

Where to send: Date sent:

Method: Mail / Overnight / Email / Fax

Additional Notes:

TASKS

PAYING THE BILLS

It's important to continue to pay the bills. In the chaos of recent weeks, it's easy to misplace bills, forget about them, etc… You want to keep your accounts current and avoid late fees and interest penalties. Aside from the penalty costs, not paying the bills can hurt your credit score.

Earlier, we asked you to make a list of the major bills. In this stage, we want you to revisit the bills and determine which ones need your attention. What do we mean by that?

If there are loans or subscriptions in your husband's name only, it's important to continue to pay them until you pay off the balance, sell the asset or cancel the subscription. If there is a large payment/expense that you need to stop as soon as possible, address it first.

Credit Cards

Did your husband have a credit card in his name only?

➡ You are not personally responsible for his charges, but his estate is. Meaning, you can't necessarily just ignore the bill and refuse to pay it off since it's not in your name.

➡ Notify the bank/card issuer of your husband's death. Make sure they freeze the account so no new charges can be made.

➡ Review the last twelve months of statements for subscription charges. We recommend going back this far because subscriptions are usually paid monthly or just once a year (annually). If an annual subscription is coming up for renewal, you want to catch it before it gets charged.

Loans

Did your husband have a car/motorcycle/boat loan or similar in his name only?

➡ You are not personally responsible for his loan(s), but his estate is. Meaning, you can't necessarily just ignore the bill and refuse to pay it off since it's not in your name.

➡ Notify the bank/lender of your husband's death. Ask for the current balance.

➡ Are you going to keep the property attached to the loan? If not, if you sell the vehicle or whatever it is, will you receive enough to pay off the loan?

TASKS

PAYING THE BILLS (CONTINUED)

Subscriptions/Memberships

Did your husband have subscriptions or membership dues that can be cancelled? Some examples:

➡ Newspapers, magazines, newsletters, books (could be print or online)

➡ Online services (i.e. Spotify, Pandora, Netflix, Apple Music, etc…)

➡ Memberships (gym, AAA, AARP, country club, pool, tennis)

➡ Retailers (Costco, BJs, Sam's Club, Amazon Prime)

Utilities

Do any of these need to be updated/changed? Note that some utility registrations are tied to a home's ownership, which means filing a new deed might be required to remove his name.

Electric   Water/Sewer   Cell Phone   Internet/Cable/Home Phone

Insurance

Did your husband have these other types of insurances? If so they can probably be cancelled before the next premium is due.

➡ Auto/home/excess liability - Cancel the policy or remove your husband as driver or insured as applicable.

➡ Disability - Cancel the policy.

➡ Long-term care - Cancel the policy if it's just your husband's. If it's a hybrid policy that offers a death benefit, you can submit a claim form to receive it. If it's a joint policy, simply notify the insurance company.

➡ Professional liability - Accountants, financial advisors, professional engineers, architects, construction trades people, etc… all carry some form of professional liability insurance that can be cancelled.

TASKS

PAYING THE BILLS (CONTINUED)

Mortgage

➡ Regardless of whose name it's in, keep paying it. All the mortgage company really cares about is receiving their payments. If you can't afford the payments, talk to an attorney about your options.

Rent

Who's name is on the lease?

➡ If it's both of you, you're liable for the rent through the end of the lease.

➡ If it's only your husband, contact the landlord and ask if you can take on the lease or start a new one (assuming you want to stay there). Your rights may be limited if you're not on the lease and the landlord wants you to vacate the property.

In Stage 4 we're going to help you review your new cash flow - your income versus your expenses - to see if any additional changes need to be made. For right now, we just want you to stay on top of everything.

When bills come in the mail, keep them all in one place - a drawer, a basket on the counter, or similar. Don't mix them with other papers or documents.

If bills, receipts or notifications come by email, create a new folder in your email software called "Bills" or similar and put the emails in the folder so it's easier to find them later.

On the next page is a table where you can keep track of your bills.

 *Not Just A Widow*

Bills & Payments Worksheet

Instructions: Use this worksheet to keep track of your bills, how often they are paid and whether it's something you can cancel. Start with large one time bills that are coming up and then work off your credit card statement or checking statement for regular bills. (You can download a digital pdf copy of this worksheet at www.notjustawidow.com/worksheets)

Description	Frequency (monthly/ quarterly/ annually)	Due Date	Amount ($)	Individual /Joint	Keep/ Cancel

TASKS

CLAIM LIFE INSURANCE DEATH BENEFITS

Regardless of whether the life insurance was through an employer (referred to as "group" insurance) or purchased directly from an insurance company via an agent or broker, the claims process is the same. The insurance company will have a benefit claim form that needs to be completed and submitted with the certified death certificate.

There are a number of ways to contact the insurance company and notify them of your husband's passing:

➡ If you have a relationship with the insurance agent who sold the policy, call them and they will help you through the process.

➡ You can usually go to the insurance company's web site and download a digital pdf copy of the form.

➡ You can call the phone number on your statement or on the web site and ask the service person for the forms.

Once the forms are submitted, you'll usually have a couple of options regarding receiving the money. The insurance company can send a check made out to the beneficiary of the policy. The beneficiary then deposits the money into their checking or savings account.

Alternatively, the insurance company will usually offer an account that earns interest and provides you checks for paying bills and accessing the account.

One thing that often confuses people about life insurance proceeds is the income taxes. Life insurance proceeds are not subject to income taxes. Once those proceeds are deposited into an account that earns interest, the interest is usually taxable.

LIFE INSURANCE DEATH BENEFIT SUMMARY

We've included a couple of tables below for you to write down information about your husband's life insurance policies to make it easier to keep track of the claims process.

Life Insurance Summary	
Company Name	
Agent Name	
Phone Number	
Policy Number	
Death Benefit	
Beneficiary	
Have copy of policy?	
Date Claim Submitted	
Date Benefit Received	

Life Insurance Summary	
Company Name	
Agent Name	
Phone Number	
Policy Number	
Death Benefit	
Beneficiary	
Have copy of policy?	
Date Claim Submitted	
Date Benefit Received	

We hate to say it, but you need to be very careful with life insurance agents and financial advisors who sell insurance. Because they earn large commissions from the sale of insurance products, they are tempted to sell you new insurance products using the proceeds from your husband's policy - especially annuities promising guaranteed income and the like. We've seen it first hand. We suggest you do not purchase any additional life insurance or other insurance products for a number of months or longer unless there are extenuating circumstances. Wait for your situation to stabilize and for that "brain fog" to lift. You may need that money for something else.

TASKS

DOCUMENT WEB SITE AND EMAIL LOGIN INFORMATION

Almost everyone has an online presence. Now is a good time to make a list of all your husband's email addresses, social media accounts and frequently visited web sites.

➡ Most web sites, but especially financial web sites, forbid anyone other than the registered user from using the log in information. Violating this rule voids privacy and identity theft protections, so tread carefully.

Description	Web or Email Address	User ID	Password

Not Just A Widow Guidebook

STAGE 3 CONTENTS

"Hold Onto The Love, Not The Loss"

INTRODUCTION

Stage 3 starts roughly two months after your husband's death and lasts four months or so. At the beginning of the stage, you are still in "The Fog". The grief is still new, it's raw, it's overwhelming. Your sleeping habits are probably shot. You may not be eating properly. You're just going through the motions.

This is when reality starts to set in that you are now on your own, and that can be very scary. What are you going to do? How will you get through this? At some point, you will probably have an "episode" where you look back and point to it as a turning point in your healing. It will be a major and dramatic release of pent-up stress and emotion. Let it come; it's part of the healing process.

As hard as it is to believe, trust us when we say: You will get through this. It will take time, but you are already transforming into your new you. Give her time to show herself. There's no need to rush things.

We'll also look at a number of important tasks you will likely need to address. Remember to ask for help if you feel overwhelmed.

After the first couple of months, I was still completely in "The Fog". The reality of Basil's death hadn't totally sunk in. I remember a trigger - that had nothing to do with my husband or his death - that caused me to break down and give in to the grief at around week eight. I cried and I wailed and I totally lost it.

But afterwards, I felt a bit of a reawakening. There is still "The Fog", but it isn't as thick. The grief episodes continued - usually triggered by something that reminded me of Basil. For me they seemed to happen most frequently in the grocery store or when I was driving. As the weeks went by, they happened less frequently, but even a year later there were moments of intense grief that washed over me.

Before the episode I couldn't even think of doing anything beyond the most basic of tasks, but afterwards I gradually felt more clear-headed. I began tackling the various administrative and financial planning tasks that every widow has to deal with.

I remember feeling some anger at my situation. I felt self-pity. Why me? I didn't deserve this. Learning to accept this new reality took time. It took about six months before I was ready to talk about Basil's death with anyone. As many widows find, attending a grief workshop or counseling session with other widows was a major turning point for me. After trying some groups that just didn't seem to click, and with the holidays looming, I saw a posting for a workshop called *Surviving Your First Holiday Alone*. I decided to give it a shot and it was one of the best decisions I've made. I met some wonderful widow sisters there, and together we got each other through the tough days. We talk much more about this in Stage 4.

PATTY'S SISTERLY ADVICE

L ooking back on those early months (after the first couple of months), I remember things slowly getting better.

➡ Early on, you will have a "good day" amongst a lot of "bad days". You may find it difficult to laugh or smile.

➡ Initially, it may seem like everything triggers a wave of despair or grief. That slowly and gradually lessens. It can easily take a year or more before the grief episodes are few and far between.

➡ It's natural to miss the intimacy you shared with your husband and to be disappointed when another man can't provide it.

➡ Remember that everyone is different and every widow's journey is her own. Go at your own pace and ignore those people who put expectations on how you are feeling. Unless they've been through it themselves, these people don't understand that your life has been upended.

COBRA - The acronym for the law that allows an eligible employee or his or her dependents to continue health insurance coverage after that employee loses his job. The law was the Consolidated Omnibus Budget Reconciliation Act, which was passed in 1985.

INSURANCE MARKETPLACE - A place for people to buy health insurance outside of an employer. Someone might use an insurance marketplace because their employer doesn't offer health insurance, they are a part-time employee and don't qualify to purchase it through their employer, they are currently unemployed, they are self-employed, etc…

MEDICAID - The federal program administered through the states that provides free or low cost health coverage to people. Qualifications are largely based on income and are state specific.

MEDICARE - The federal program that provides health insurance for Americans age 65 and older. In the United States, where health insurance has historically been provided by employers, Medicare was created for retirees.

MEDICARE PART A - The portion of Medicare that covers hospitals, skilled nursing and hospice services. This is the part paid for by the money withheld from a worker's paycheck.

MEDICARE PART B - The portion of Medicare that covers outpatient services, office visits and doctor/nurse administered prescription drugs. Retirees pay a premium for Part B, most often via a deduction from their Social Security benefit.

ASSET - As asset is something you own. It can be a physical piece of property or it can be something that only exists on paper or in a computer database, like a stock share.

LIABILITY - A liability is a debt. It's something you owe. A credit card balance, a car loan, and a mortgage are all liabilities.

CREDITOR - The person or business from whom someone has borrowed money.

DECEDENT - The legal term for a person who has died.

TITLE - Who owns an asset and what type of ownership is it? How is it "titled"? Common forms of title are individual, joint tenants with right of survivorship (JTWROS), joint tenants in the entirety, tenants in common, trust, estate, partnership.

WILL - The legal document where a person names a Personal Representative, how their property should be distributed and, if there are minor children, who should be their guardian.

PROBATE - This is the legal term for the process of determining if a decedent had a Will, if it is valid, naming a Personal Representative/Executor and distributing the decedent's probate property.

INTESTATE - The legal term for when a person dies without a valid Will.

PERSONAL REPRESENTATIVE/EXECUTOR - The name for the person who is responsible for settling the probate estate, which includes notifying creditors, opening a checking account for the estate (if there is income paid to the decedent after his death), and distributing any probate property.

LETTERS OF ADMINISTRATION - The name for the official document the Personal Representative uses to legally inform other parties that they are authorized to act on behalf of the decedent's estate.

BENEFICIARY - The person or persons to whom property is to be distributed upon the owner's death. The property goes directly to the beneficiary(ies) and is not part of the probate estate.

COPING WITH LOSS: YEARNING AND ANGER

Bereavement means "deprived by loss". In Stage 2, we discussed "The Fog" and some of the symptoms you might experience in the early days. In particular, many recent widows describe a sense of emotional numbness.

As the numbness recedes, you may start to feel a sense of yearning. You miss your husband, his physical presence. The house feels empty without him.

Some people have difficulty being alone as a result. Some people describe "seeing" their husband everywhere they go. It's a trick of the mind as it adjusts to the absence of someone who was such a large part of your life.

These things are all normal and common.

Have you felt angry yet? Angry with the doctors and nurses who didn't prevent your husband's death? If someone "caused" his death, anger towards that person is perfectly natural. Angry at your husband for leaving you? For putting you in this situation?

These feelings are completely normal and are a part of the grieving and healing process.

In these early days, you may not be ready to talk to people about what happened or what you are feeling. But it can be very cathartic to "get some things off your chest"…

Some widows find it helpful to keep a journal for this purpose, which is why we include a Grief Journal in each stage.

In the weeks after your husband's death you're likely going to experience wild mood swings. You may be out somewhere, see a reminder of your husband and suddenly burst into tears. It may be awkward, but you can't stop the tears. Let them flow!! They are tears of healing.

Most people won't know how to react to your tears. That's ok. They don't know what you are feeling. You may feel embarrassed or awkward if you are at work or in a public space when the tears come. This is normal. Remember you are not alone. Your sisters have been through this. Here are some of the things other widows experienced.

COPING WITH LOSS: SURVIVORSHIP GUILT

During your grieving you are going to experience a wide range of emotions. You may feel anger, sadness, confusion, and even guilt. You may feel like you should have done something "more" or differently for your husband. You may think you need to suffer because you are the one who survived. You are here - and he is gone.

These feelings are natural. Other widows have felt them as well. Allow yourself to process these feelings. As you come to accept your husband's death, the anger and guilt goes away.

COPING WITH LOSS: YOUR CHILDREN'S GRIEF

If you have children, you're in a common situation for widows, but with its own set of challenges. If you have minor children, you are now a single parent and caregiver. You may need help with childcare now. Remember that your children are also grieving the loss of their father and depending on their age they will process it in different ways. As a mother, you'll want to protect and shield your children, but you should let them experience their grief in their own way. Talk to your children about what they are feeling and what you are feeling. Even very small children, who you may think can't process the loss of their father will feed off of and react to your grief and stress. We humans are more connected than we appreciate sometimes.

WHEN TO SEEK PROFESSIONAL GRIEF COUNSELING

Women generally do a better job of sharing their feelings than men do. When talking to your friends and family members about how you are feeling in the wake of your husband's death, be aware that it's common for your support system to get weary of you talking about your loss. Talking about death is uncomfortable and can be stressful for many people. This is where a therapist or counselor can be an important tool to assist in your healing.

Where there used to be a stigma associated with seeing a mental health professional, that is no longer the case (nor should it be). If you are struggling to cope with your loss, here are some places to look for help:

➡ Individual counselors, including psychiatrists, psychologists, and grief therapists

➡ Religious organizations that offer grief counseling

➡ Hospices

➡ Grief groups (which we discuss in Stage 4)

Some counselors are providing therapy via the phone or internet, so you don't even need to leave the house or find someone local.

Some signs you may need a therapist:

➡ Trouble completing daily tasks

➡ Drinking or taking drugs to escape the grief

➡ Trouble believing that your husband is dead

➡ Others expressing concern for your welfare

➡ Unrelenting depression

➡ Uncontrollable crying on a frequent basis that isn't lessening

Experts agree that it can be therapeutic to write your thoughts and/or experiences down on paper. The process of writing is more important than what you actually write down. We have provided space below for you to express yourself however you see fit.

YOUR GRIEF JOURNAL

TASK OUTLINE

In months 2-6 after your husband's death, the tasks you should focus on begin with investigating health insurance and gathering important information about property and accounts. Only then should you move on to estate settlement and distributing your husband's assets. We've put the tasks you should work on first at the top of the list.

✓ Investigate health insurance.

✓ Make a list of property, accounts, loans, etc…

✓ Open a new checking account.

✓ Set aside savings for emergencies or unexpected expenses.

✓ Determine beneficiaries.

✓ Start the estate settlement process.

TASKS

INVESTIGATE HEALTH INSURANCE

Health insurance is a complex topic. The first thing to confirm is the source of your current coverage. Sources include: your employer, your husband's employer, Medicare, a government marketplace or directly from an insurance company.

We'll walk you through your options depending on your current situation.

Even though health insurance coverage terminates as of your husband's date of death, there will likely be claims filed after his death. You should notify the insurer of your husband's death as soon as possible, but it is important to continue paying the premiums to keep the policy active so that those claims can be paid. After all the claims are paid, contact the insurer and terminate coverage as of his date of death. You may receive a refund of the premiums paid for the post-death coverage.

SCENARIO 1: You and your husband's health coverage is through <u>your employer.</u>

➡ Notify the insurer that your husband has died.

➡ The premium will continue to be deducted from your paycheck.

➡ At the next open enrollment, remove your husband's coverage.

SCENARIO 2: Your current health coverage is through <u>your employer;</u> his coverage was through another insurer.

➡ Your coverage remains unchanged.

➡ Notify his coverage's insurance company and continue to pay the current premium.

➡ His coverage will end after all claims are paid or at the end of the year.

SCENARIO 3: Your husband was covered under <u>Medicare.</u>

➡ Medicare is notified by the Social Security Administration. His coverage will stop. If you are over age 65, your Medicare coverage continues.

INVESTIGATE HEALTH INSURANCE (CONTINUED)

SCENARIO 4: You and your husband's coverage is through a <u>state marketplace,</u> healthcare.gov or directly with the health insurance company.

➡ Notify the health insurance company and keep paying the premiums.

➡ If you are receiving an advanced premium tax credit, you'll need to tell the state marketplace or healthcare.gov of your husband's death so that they can adjust the credit.

SCENARIO 5: Your current health coverage is through your <u>husband's employer</u>

➡ Notify human resources that you are interested in COBRA. COBRA is available if the employer has 20 or more employees.

➡ The employer was supposed to notify the health plan within 30 days of your husband's death. If you are COBRA eligible, they have 14 days to provide notice to you regarding coverage and then you have at least 60 days to elect coverage. You can continue the policy under COBRA for up to 36 months.

➡ You are likely to find that the premiums increase under COBRA versus what you were paying previously. This is because the employer was paying some of the premium as an employee benefit. Under COBRA the employer does not have to continue to subsidize those premiums.

➡ You may also qualify for some premium assistance from the federal government depending on your circumstances.

Additional information on COBRA can be found on the Centers for Medicare and Medicaid Services' web site.

https://www.cms.gov/CCIIO/Programs-and-Initiatives/Other-Insurance-Protections/cobra_qna.html

Once you initiate COBRA coverage, you can choose to stop that coverage and start other coverage if that is appropriate for your circumstances. You might start coverage at your employer or buy coverage from a state or the federal health marketplace.

HEALTH INSURANCE MARKETPLACES

People in most states use the federal government's marketplace at **healthcare.gov.** However, some states offer their own marketplace. Links to those state health insurance marketplaces are below. If your state isn't listed, then they do not offer a marketplace and you would need to shop for coverage on healthcare.gov. Since the death of a spouse is considered a qualified event, you can apply for new coverage at any time. Normally a person has to wait for open enrollment in November to apply for new coverage on the marketplaces.

California	www.coveredca.com
Colorado	www.connectforhealthco.com
Connecticut	www.accesshealthct.com
District of Columbia	www.dchealthlink.com
Idaho	www.yourhealthidaho.org
Maryland	www.marylandhealthconnection.gov
Massachusetts	www.mahealthconnector.org
Minnesota	www.mnsure.org
Nevada	www.nevadahealthlink.com
New York	www.nystateofhealth.ny.gov
Rhode Island	www.healthsourceri.com
Vermont	www.healthconnect.vermont.gov
Washington	www.wahealthplanfinder.org

TASKS

LIST PROPERTY, ACCOUNTS, LOANS, ETC...

Making an inventory of all your property/assets is an important task. Not only is it critical for financial planning purposes, it is also needed to settle your husband's estate (which we'll address later).

For each asset (the things you and your husband own), you want to know what it is, where it is, what it was worth on his date of death, how it is titled, if there is a beneficiary designation and what you paid for it.

For each loan, you want to know who took out the loan, how much is still owed and the terms (amount borrowed; interest rate; date borrowed; payment frequency; loan period).

This may sound like a lot of work - it can be depending on your situation. Trust us, this is all critical information that you, your accountant/tax preparer, attorney, and financial advisor will need in the coming weeks and months.

On the pages that follow, we've provided worksheets to keep track of critical information about all your property, accounts and loans.

➡ Not every piece of information is applicable in all cases, but the more information you can gather now will save you time and hassle later.

➡ Everyone has different skills. If this task is overwhelming, ask someone you trust to help.

➡ Any asset or loan that is in your name only won't require any immediate attention, but you might as well get current information about them while you're at it.

➡ Do not give away, gift, transfer, throw away or sell anything just yet.

Physical Property Worksheet

Instructions: This worksheet helps you gather important information about any physical property you and your husband own. This includes a house, vacation property, cars, recreation vehicles, boats, collectibles, tv, computer, watch, jewelry, etc... You don't have to list small or inexpensive items. Provide as much information as you are able for each item. (You can download a digital pdf copy of this worksheet at www.notjustawidow.com/worksheets)

Property Description:

Where is it located?

Who owns it?

Is there a deed/title?

If yes, where is it?

When was it purchased?

How much did it cost?

What is it worth now?

How did you get this value?

Was a loan used to buy it?

If yes, do you still owe money on the loan? If yes, complete a Loan Worksheet. If no, do you have a copy of the loan payoff letter and/or the updated title (if applicable)? _____ YES/NO

Additional Information:

Physical Property Worksheet

Instructions: This worksheet helps you gather important information about any physical property you and your husband own. This includes a house, vacation property, cars, recreation vehicles, boats, collectibles, tv, computer, watch, jewelry, etc... You don't have to list small or inexpensive items. Provide as much information as you are able for each item. (You can download a digital pdf copy of this worksheet at www.notjustawidow.com/worksheets)

Property Description:

Where is it located?

Who owns it?

Is there a deed/title?

If yes, where is it?

When was it purchased?

How much did it cost?

What is it worth now?

How did you get this value?

Was a loan used to buy it?

If yes, do you still owe money on the loan? If yes, complete a Loan Worksheet. If no, do you have a copy of the loan payoff letter and/or the updated title (if applicable)? _____ YES/NO

Additional Information:

Financial Account Worksheet

Account Type:

Bank/Financial Firm/Insurance Co:

Account number:

Ownership:

Do you have a recent statement?

Is a beneficiary/POD/TOD named? Who?

Value on your husband's date of death?

What is it worth now?

Does it receive automatic deposits or make auto distributions? How much?

Do you have the most recent tax forms for this account? (i.e. 1099 or 5498)

Additional Information:

Financial Account Worksheet

Instructions: This worksheet helps you gather important information about any financial accounts you and your husband own. This includes checking, savings, CDs, money markets, IRAs, employer retirement plans, annuities, savings bonds, mutual fund accounts, brokerage accounts, stocks, etc... Provide as much information as you are able to for each account. (You can download a digital pdf copy of this worksheet at www.notjustawidow.com/worksheets)

Account Type:

Bank/Financial Firm/Insurance Co:

Account number:

Ownership:

Do you have a recent statement?

Is a beneficiary/POD/TOD named? Who?

Value on your husband's date of death?

What is it worth now?

Does it receive automatic deposits or make auto distributions? How much?

Do you have the most recent tax forms for this account? (i.e. 1099 or 5498)

Additional Information:

Not Just A Widow

Loan Worksheet

Instructions: This worksheet helps you gather important information about any loans or lines of credit you and your husband have. This includes a mortgage, home equity loan or line of credit, car or other vehicle loan, student loan, home improvement loan, credit cards, bank loans, etc... Provide as much information as you are able to for each account. (You can download a digital pdf copy of this worksheet at www.notjustawidow.com/worksheets)

Loan Type:

Bank/Lender:

Account number:

Borrower(s):

What was the loan used to buy?

When was the loan taken out?

What is the loan period?

Original amount borrowed:

How much is still owed?

Interest rate: (variable or fixed?)

Are monthly payments required? How much?

Additional Information:

Loan Worksheet

Instructions: This worksheet helps you gather important information about any loans or lines of credit you and your husband have. This includes a mortgage, home equity loan or line of credit, car or other vehicle loan, student loan, home improvement loan, credit cards, bank loans, etc... Provide as much information as you are able to for each account. (You can download a digital pdf copy of this worksheet at www.notjustawidow.com/worksheets)

Loan Type:

Bank/Lender:

Account number:

Borrower(s):

What was the loan used to buy?

When was the loan taken out?

What is the loan period?

Original amount borrowed:

How much is still owed?

Interest rate: (variable or fixed?)

Are monthly payments required? How much?

Additional Information:

STAGE 3

TASKS

SET UP A NEW CHECKING ACCOUNT

At this stage - before you do any estate settlement - we don't suggest widows make any changes to any accounts that had their husband's name on it. Don't remove your husband's name from an account or add a child's name to an account. Don't close any of your husband's accounts. Often, widows will receive a check or rebate or some other income item after their husband has passed and they need an account with his name on it to make the deposit.

We do recommend that you have a checking account in your name only, if you don't have one already.

➡ Open the new checking account at the same bank where the primary joint checking account is. It will make it easier to transfer money when needed.

➡ Deposit any money you receive into your checking account. Try not to commingle this money in a joint checking account you had with your husband. It complicates the estate settlement process.

➡ If you had any direct deposits to a joint checking (like a paycheck or Social Security benefits), switch them to your individual checking account.

TASKS

SET UP AN EMERGENCY FUND

In the early weeks and months, life is chaotic - emotionally, socially, financially. We suggest not making any long term plans during the early stages because so much can and will change.

We recommend that you keep as much money "liquid" as you can. Liquid means easily accessible. If you have a surprise expense, you want to be able pay for it without selling anything, paying a penalty, etc…

Here are some things to consider regarding where to keep your Emergency Funds:

➡ Savings/Money Market Account

- ◉ FDIC coverage is $250,000 per person. Coverage can be boosted by adding beneficiaries (also called a P.O.D. - Payable On Death).

- ◉ Look for high yielding options on bankrate.com. They will likely be internet based banks since they don't have the costs associated with having local branches.

➡ Money Market at brokerage firm

- ◉ SIPC coverage is $250,000 for the "core cash" portion of the account. Large firms often provide additional coverage.

- ◉ Link the brokerage account to your checking account so you can electronically transfer money back and forth as needed.

➡ Retained Asset accounts from life insurance proceeds

- ◉ When receiving life insurance proceeds, the insurance companies offer you an interest bearing account and check writing. You don't have to keep the money there and can deposit the funds into a bank account that offers FDIC coverage and a higher interest rate.

DETERMINE BENEFICIARIES

A beneficiary is the person (or people/charities) that the account owner has named to receive all or a portion of the account (or asset) upon their death. Many assets/accounts can have one or more beneficiaries named. The most common types of accounts that have beneficiaries named are life insurance and retirement plans/IRAs. Bank accounts and brokerage/mutual fund accounts can have them also (but often don't). Some states now allow home owners to name beneficiaries.

The beneficiary receives the asset or money directly from the institution after completing a claim form and providing a death certificate. These assets are not part of the probate estate.

Just because it's possible to name a beneficiary, it doesn't mean that one was named. When no beneficiary is named, the account/asset is paid to the decedent's probate estate and then the Will dictates where the money/asset goes from there.

Some additional insight regarding accounts with beneficiaries:

➡ Expect some frustration when dealing with financial institutions. Modern privacy rules and security concerns mean that customer service representatives might not give you the names of beneficiaries or they will make it difficult to get the information.

➡ Life insurance proceeds you receive as beneficiary are not taxable income.

➡ If you inherit a Traditional IRA or retirement plan (versus a Roth IRA or Roth 401(k)), all or most of that money will be included as taxable income on your tax return when you take a distribution. Make sure you plan for paying the income tax liability if you withdraw money from an IRA or retirement plan.

TASKS

SETTLE HIS ESTATE

This part of the process can be frustrating and confusing. The financial and legal terms and processes are unfamiliar to most people. The list of property and accounts we suggested you create will be very helpful as you work through your husband's accounts. It's very difficult to provide any sort of general advice when it comes to settling an estate. Everything you do is dependent on the particulars of the asset.

Ask lots of questions, take notes, and get professional help if you need it.

Do you need to open an estate for your husband? What does this mean?

➡ The city/town/township/county where your husband lived will have a "Registrar of Wills" or "probate judge" or similar type government official. If in doubt, call the general switchboard for your local government, tell them your husband passed and ask which office handles "probate and Wills".

➡ This is a slight simplification, but the probate process exists for those cases where a decedent hasn't otherwise left instructions for how to disburse their assets. If there isn't a joint owner, a beneficiary named, or a trust in place, then the Will dictates disbursement. If there's no Will, the state's intestate laws dictate the disbursement rules.

➡ While your husband's overall estate includes everything he owned, his <u>probate</u> estate only includes property and assets that don't pass directly to an heir. This confuses everyone, so here are some examples:

   ⦿ You and your husband have a joint checking account. Half of the account value is part of his overall estate, but none of it is part of his probate estate. This is because you are joint owner and, by law, his half automatically becomes yours upon his death.

   ⦿ Your husband owns a life insurance policy that names you as beneficiary. The death benefit is part of his overall estate, but it is not part of his probate estate. By law, the money goes directly to you as beneficiary.

   ⦿ Your husband owns a car or other vehicle titled only in his name. It is part of his overall estate and it is part of his probate estate. His Will dictates to whom the car should be given. You can't sell or transfer it until you or who ever is named as personal representative open your husband's probate estate and get Letters of Administration or similar.

TASKS

SETTLE HIS ESTATE (CONTINUED)

➡ The first questions that the government office that handles probate will most likely ask you are:

- ◉ Did your husband have a Will? They will want a copy of the Will so they can record it and confirm that it meets the requirements of the state.

- ◉ What was the value of your husband's estate? They are specifically referring to probate estate property. Most states have a simplified estate settlement process for "small" estates. Each state defines what a "small" estate is.

- ◉ If you have your property and account list, you can show it to the official and they can help you determine what, if any, property is part of the probate estate.

➡ If you have to open a probate estate, this is generally the process:

- ◉ File the Will with the government official and they review it.

- ◉ Who ever is named Personal Representative/Executor in the Will (usually the spouse) is issued Letters of Administration or a similarly titled document. This is the document that officially gives the Personal Representative/Executor the power to do what they need to do.

- ◉ The Personal Representative goes to the IRS's web site and gets a tax identification number (like a Social Security Number) for the estate.

- ◉ The Personal Representative goes to a bank and opens an estate checking account.

- ◉ The Personal Representative starts retitling property, paying off debts, closing accounts, etc…

- ◉ There will be forms to file along the way and a final accounting to the government.

TASKS

SETTLE HIS ESTATE (CONTINUED)

➡ The time it takes to settle an estate depends on how complex it is.

- ◉ A small estate with a few bank accounts and limited personal property may be settled in a few months.

- ◉ If a house needs to be sold or have the title transferred, this can extend estate settlement for months.

- ◉ If your husband owned a business, investment real estate or other complicated types of assets, settlement could takes months or years.

- ◉ A large estate with complex assets included in the probate estate or that has a trust can easily take over a year to settle.

➡ Do you need help? How do you find it?

- ◉ A fee-only financial advisor (someone who doesn't sell insurance or investment products) can help you catalogue property and debts and understand your overall circumstances on an hourly or fixed fee basis.

- ◉ Some accountant/tax preparers can help you review your income tax return for accounts that generate income.

- ◉ A local attorney that practices different types of law can help you register a Will, open an estate, deal with banks and other financial institutions, etc… Make sure they charge an hourly or fixed fee versus taking a percentage of the estate's value.

- ◉ An estate attorney is one who specializes in complex estates and trusts and tax laws. Very few people need this type of help, but for those that do, an estate attorney is invaluable. They are also very expensive.

Not Just A Widow Guidebook

Stage 4 Contents

"One Step At A Time, One Moment At A Time"

INTRODUCTION

We define Stage 4 as that open ended space of time that starts roughly six months after his passing and extends a year or more. This is a period of internal change for most widows. You are beginning to experience life without your husband. What does that mean?

Activities you did together don't feel the same. If you did a lot of "couple" activities, you are now the single person and it feels awkward. As a parent, the role you play may shift.

You will start this stage by exploring new friends, new activities, and a new sense of self. You will continue to grieve. You will experience frustration as not everything works out. It's ok if you don't have all the answers. Give yourself time to heal and to adjust to your new world.

During this time, you may face some major decisions. You may find it necessary to change jobs or start a new job. You may find that your current residence isn't a good fit. You will probably review your income and expenses. Take your time when making these big decisions since your life is still in flux.

PATTY'S SISTERLY ADVICE

Time seems like it's passing quickly and then some days it drags. At this point, carving out your new life no matter how hard it may be is essential to your well-being. This is the point where you realize many people don't understand what you are feeling. You are tired of "the head tilt", the "pathetic" look and the awkwardness when someone learns your husband died.

But there are people who understand what you are feeling; who will respect the rawness of those feelings; who won't treat you with pity. They are your sisters - fellow widows who are there to support you.

When I started to look for grief groups, the first few were not a good fit. That's ok. There are many different groups because widows come from all sorts of backgrounds. You may be surprised by how you never knew about all these women united by their common experience. It's one of the ironic things about widowhood - no married woman wants to think about her husband's death - but there are literally millions of widows the world over. You are not alone.

Form new relationships with the sisterhood. Find like-minded women and talk to them. Find out how they carved out their new life.

As my first holiday season without Basil loomed large, I found a grief workshop titled "Surviving the first holiday alone". It was a weekly group and there were about ten women there. It turned out to be a perfect fit for me.

In fact, after the six week class ended, five of us decided to continue meeting. We called ourselves the WITs - Women In Transition. That's what we were. We would get together for lunch, dinner, a movie, visit wineries, travel. We helped each other through sickness. We got it. The sisterhood.

Nine years later and the WITs are still together. We cannot be broken, and the support has been phenomenal.

There is life for you after the passing of your husband. You just need to put one foot in front of the other and keep moving forward. Regardless of what your life becomes or what else you do in life you are forever labelled a widow. That's okay. It's just how it is. Remember you are not JUST a widow.

You might be surprised by how your address book changes after your spouse passes away. Your relationship with certain family members may change - especially his family. Most widows I've spoken with tell me they've lost some friends and also found some new ones.

It can feel weird to make major decisions entirely by yourself. Before, you and your husband did that as a team. It may take some time to get used to that. You'll build up your confidence over time. Don't hesitate to ask for opinions or insight, but remember that you have to do what's best for you, your children if you have them and your future.

Baby steps are ok. It's ok to try something and change your mind. Your journey will likely take years and that's normal and typical.

GROSS EARNINGS/PAY - Income or earnings before any taxes or other deductions are taken out.

NET EARNINGS/PAY - Also referred to "take home", this is what's left after tax and other deductions are taken out of a person's paycheck.

QUALIFYING WIDOW - The IRS filing status that is available to widows with dependent children for the two years following the year her husband died.

HEAD OF HOUSEHOLD - The IRS filing status that is available to single parents with dependent children.

DEPENDENT - The IRS has formal rules for how to determine if a person qualifies as a dependent for income tax purposes. These include reviewing the person's relationship to you, whether they lived with you over the last year, their age and who provided their "support" (food/clothing/shelter).

CHANGING RELATIONSHIPS

It is common for some of your relationships to change as a result of your husband's death. Ask any widow and she will likely have a story about how she was surprised by how a person in her life reacted, how she lost touch with a close friend or family member or how the experience deepened her relationship with someone. You never can tell how people will react to you and your new reality. Be prepared for some changes.

FEAR OF GETTING SICK

One of the things we routinely hear from widows is that they have a heightened sense of anxiousness surrounding getting sick versus before their husband passed. Couples rely on their partners to be there for them when they need to get a procedure done or are just feeling under the weather. If you are feeling nervous about this, it's normal and common. Widows with children often come to rely on them more and, if you don't have children or they live far from you, make sure you connect with your local sisters so you can support one another.

YOUR HUSBAND'S BELONGINGS

One of the surreal experiences of widowhood is dealing with your husband's personal belongings. From his socks, to his toothbrush, to his collection of whatever he collected. Each widow's situation is unique and how you work through his belongings will be your personal decision. Most widows find it takes time. Don't rush to give anything away. How you feel about certain belongings may change over time. Something that is a painful reminder now may become a fond memory two years from now.

Widow Story: "I had heard the stories of people who didn't tackle this task relatively quickly and wound up facing it a year or years later, and I didn't want that to be my experience. Within weeks after my husband's death, my sister, daughter and I thoughtfully sorted through his things. His World Cup soccer jerseys went to my brother who shared my husband's enthusiasm about the sport; his favorite Jimi Hendrix t-shirt went to a nephew who is a musician; his favorite leather jacket was sent to his brother; my daughter and I picked out some of our favorite things. Then I had my sister take his suits and other clothes to a charity. I, personally, could not make that trip alone with all his things around me in the car. That would have been too hard for me."

Widow Story: "I returned to work about two weeks after the funeral and found it therapeutic. The part of my brain that had to focus on work allowed the grieving side of my brain to rest."

Widow Story: "I moved two years after my husband's death for practical reasons -- the house was too big for me and my daughter was heading to college. I also had a long commute to work that was always irritating. As I did so, though, I understood why it could be hard for others to leave a long-time home with so many memories. In hindsight, I am glad I did it because it occurred to me that those memories might have trapped me there and thwarted the need for me to move on with my life. "

FINDING OTHER WIDOWS LOCALLY

Even if you are looking for a local group, the internet is an incredible tool you can use to find people (as you already know). Of course, in a world as vast as the internet, it can be hard to find what you're looking for sometimes. Below and on the next few pages we've provided some ideas for how to find a group of sisters to connect with.

If you type "city/town/county widow's group" (i.e. "Baltimore widow's group") or "city/town/county widow's support group" (i.e. "Baltimore widow's support group") you will get a long list of local resources.

Funeral Homes – Local funeral homes can be outstanding resources for the newly widowed. They always offer a list of resources for widows on their web sites. They may also offer outreach services or aftercare.

ModernWidowsClub - This is a fairly new group founded by a widow in 2011. They have a rapidly expanding local chapter base where you can connect with your sisters. Their web site is www.modernwidowsclub.com.

Churches - They often provide grief and bereavement groups and "Griefshare" sponsored groups.

MeetUp groups - These can be helpful if you are looking for a social outlet.

Hospices - May offer grief and bereavement counseling and support. If you search "city/town hospices", you will find them. A trip to their web site will indicate the support services they offer.

Cancer Centers - If your husband died of cancer, the local cancer hospital or treatment center may have support services. Search their web site for more information.

Active Military - If your husband was an active military service member, there are services available at your local base.

ONLINE RESOURCES

There are two great benefits of the internet - learning about something and connecting with someone who isn't geographically close to you. For widows, this is especially true. You can find other women who are not only widows, but also whose personal circumstances are similar to yours. For example, you can find other widows who are of the same age, have children or don't, work outside the home or don't, etc...

Many widows have done what Patty has done - turned the tragedy of their husband's death - into a positive way to help other women. They have written books, created web sites and started organizations.

On our web site, **www.notjustawidow.com**, we have a list of online resources where you can read about other widows' experiences and how they coped with the grief and overcame challenges. They run the gamut from a single woman's experiences to a place where widows can come together to support one another. Below is a sample of some web sites.

➡ *Soaring Spirits International* is a large organization with a number of different resources for widows.

   ◉ www.soaringspirits.org

   ◉ Widowed Village- An online community where you can connect with other widows.

   ◉ Camp Widow- Soaring Spirits' provider of workshops and camps.

   ◉ Widow's Voice Blog- A blog that posts helpful information for widows.

➡ The Sisterhood of Widows was founded by Mary Francis, a Certified Grief Recovery Specialist and she has authored a number of grief books, which are available on her site. www.sisterhoodofwidows.com

➡ Tragedy Assistance Program for Survivors (TAPS) is an organization that supports the families after the death of a military loved one. www.taps.org

FACEBOOK GROUPS

Facebook is an incredible resource for connecting with likeminded individuals. While most groups are "open" to anyone who wants to join, there are also "closed" groups that provide more privacy. This is especially attractive for widows who want to ensure they are only interacting with other widows.

There are specialty groups that may focus on your specific circumstances. For example, if you are a widow with small children or if your husband died in a tragic accident.

Not Just a Widow has a Facebook page where you can find lists and links to widow resources and groups. You can find us be searching for "Not Just A Widow Guidebook".

Some groups you may be interested in:

➡ Widowed for Widowed

➡ Widowed Women Over 50 - Moving Forward

➡ For Widows Only

➡ Young Widows and Widowers Support Group

➡ Forever After

Experts agree that it can be therapeutic to write your thoughts and/or experiences down on paper. The process of writing is more important than what you actually write down. We have provided space below for you to express yourself however you see fit.

YOUR GRIEF JOURNAL

TASK OUTLINE

In months 6-18 after your husband's death, the tasks you should focus on begin with understanding your cash flow. If the income won't support the expenses, where will the money come from? Life insurance may provide a temporary solution to a cash flow problem, but you don't want to spend all that money if you might need it in the future. We've put the tasks you should work on first at the top of the list. We explain each task on the pages that follow. If you've completed the tasks we've set out for you previously, it will make these tasks easier.

✓ Create a Budget and Calculate Cash Flow.

✓ Review Employment.

✓ Filing Income Tax Returns.

✓ Examine Housing.

CREATE A BUDGET & CALCULATE CASH FLOW

Almost every widow is going to experience a change to her income and expenses. If your husband was still working, his salary stops. If he was retired and receiving Social Security and/or a pension, those amounts may be changing. You need to adjust; you need to make decisions. In order to make good decisions, you need good information. If you don't feel confident working through your new budget, have a trusted friend help or hire a fee-only financial planner. Either way, you need to gather information about your income and expenses. We've included some worksheets if you want to do this yourself or with a friend. Financial planners usually have their own tools.

Income Worksheet - We recommend compiling a list of the household income before your husband passed and then noting how that income has changed. We also recommend grabbing a copy of last year's income tax return and its associated worksheets and supporting forms since all your income will be listed there.

Expense Worksheet - We've broken up expenses between the housing worksheet and the personal expenses worksheet. Often, housing expenses are a household's largest after income taxes. Housing expenses also can change significantly between two residences. Personal expenses can be tougher to track and can be very different from month to month.

Cash Flow Needs - Add up the income and subtract all the expenses to arrive at your new annual cash flow figure. If the number is negative, how will you "fill the gap?" How long can you fill the gap before changes need to be made?

Current Income Worksheet

Instructions: This worksheet helps you gather important information about your current income sources. We've listed the most common ones, but feel free to add any others you might have. Budgeting is best done on a monthly basis, so convert each item to monthly if it isn't already paid that way. (You can download a digital pdf copy of this worksheet at www.notjustawidow.com/worksheets)

Description	Monthly Amount
Take Home Pay............................	$_____
Side jobs/Consulting...................	$_____
Social Security Benefits...............	$_____
Pension......................................	$_____
Annuity/Insurance Benefits.........	$_____
Interest (savings; CDs; bonds)...........	$_____
Dividends (stocks; mutual funds)...........	$_____
Retirement Plan/IRA Distribution	$_____
Other	$_____
Other	$_____
Other	$_____
Other	$_____
Other	$_____
Other	$_____
Other	$_____
TOTAL:	$_____

Not Just A Widow

Housing Expense Worksheet

Instructions: Household budgeting is a complicated process. If you don't use software or an app, these expense worksheets are a good place to start. Budgeting is best done on a monthly basis, so convert each item to monthly even if you don't pay it that way. (Get digital copies of this worksheet at www.notjustawidow.com/worksheets)

Description	Monthly Amount
Mortgage/Rent......................................	$_____
Home Equity Loan................................	$_____
Property Tax... (if not part of mortgage payment)	$_____
Homeowner/Renter Insurance.............. (if not part of mortgage payment)	$_____
Electric/Gas/Oil....................................	$_____
Water/Sewer...	$_____
Phone..	$_____
Cable/Internet......................................	$_____
HOA/Condo Assc/Co-Op Fees.............	$_____
Upkeep & Repairs.................................	$_____
Other	$_____
Other	$_____
Other	$_____
Housing Expense TOTAL:	$_____

Personal Expense Worksheet

Instructions: Household budgeting is a complicated process. If you don't use software or an app, these expense worksheets are a good place to start. Budgeting is best done on a monthly basis, so convert each item to monthly even if you don't pay it that way. Watch for expenses that were your husband's and won't continue. Most Americans use credit cards to pay for the routine expenses (versus cash) and then make a monthly credit card payment. You should examine those expenses, but you don't need the details for this worksheet. (Get digital copies of this worksheet at www.notjustawidow.com/worksheets)

Description	Monthly Amount
Auto Loan/Lease..	$_____
Auto Loan/Lease..	$_____
Auto Insurance...	$_____
Insurance Premiums...................................... (life, disability, long-term care paid directly)	$_____
Medical Expenses... (premiums, deductibles, and expenses paid out-of-pocket)	$_____
Loan Payment... (include description)	$_____
Loan Payment... (include description)	$_____
Loan Payment... (include description)	$_____
Credit Card Payment..................................... (average of last 6 payments)	$_____
Credit Card Payment..................................... (average of last 6 payments)	$_____
Credit Card Payment..................................... (average of last 6 payments)	$_____
Other	$_____
Other	
Personal Expense TOTAL:	$_____

Monthly Cash Flow Worksheet

Instructions: Household budgeting is a complicated process. If you don't use software or an app, these expense worksheets are a good place to start. Use the figures you calculated from the income and expense worksheets to see how your cash flow looks. If it's positive, that's great. But most widows will end up with a negative number and you'll have to look for ways to cut expenses. (Get digital copies of worksheet at www.notjustawidow.com/worksheets)

Monthly Income Total: .... $_____

SUBTRACT Monthly Housing Expenses Total: $_____

SUBTRACT Monthly Personal Expenses Total: $_____

Monthly Cash Flow TOTAL: $_____

How Long Will The Money Last?

Money in checking/savings/CDs/money markets and other safe accounts: $_____

Divide the number above by your cash flow total to see how long your savings will last: _____ Months

TASKS

REVIEW EMPLOYMENT

In the process of reviewing your finances, you may find a change in employment is in order. Here are some of the common reasons widows look for a new job.

➡ You need more income. If your husband worked, you may need to replace some or all of his income.

➡ You need affordable health insurance. We've previously talked about COBRA coverage or getting health insurance through a state or the federal marketplace. This may only be a temporary solution. If your current employer is small and doesn't offer health insurance, or if you are working part-time and don't qualify for access to health coverage, you may need to change jobs.

➡ You need to work closer to home. When both spouses work, often one spouse ends up with a longer commute. If that was you, your new circumstances may dictate a job closer to home. Maybe you have children and you need to be closer to meet their needs. Maybe you're just tired of a long commute.

TASKS

FILING INCOME TAX RETURNS

Income taxes are rarely something that anyone wants to do, but they must be done. We recommend meeting with a tax preparer to get a better understanding of what you need to do, but in the meantime, here are some things to consider.

➡ If your husband died at the end of the year and you're fast approaching the April 15th tax filing deadline, know that you can easily file an extension that gives you another six moths. File for free at the IRS's web site, www.IRS.gov and search for "extension" in the search bar.

➡ You will file a joint return for the year your husband died. On that return, you'll check a box that tells the IRS your husband died. The years after his year of death, you'll file as single, or Qualified Widower or Head of Household if you have qualifying dependents.

➡ You may need to file a federal income tax return for your husband's estate if he received income after his death. Consult a tax professional to see if this applies to you.

➡ You may need to file a federal estate tax return for your husband if his assets were valued at over a few hundred thousand dollars. Very few Americans pay federal estate tax under the current laws, but sometimes a "notice filing" is recommended. This is a complex topic, so again, ask a qualified tax preparer or financial planner if this is something you need to look at more closely.

➡ State income tax returns are filed separately from the federal return (if you live outside of Alaska, Florida, Nevada, New Hampshire, South Dakota, Tennessee, Texas, Washington, or Wyoming).

➡ Each state has different estate and/or inheritance tax laws. Consult your tax professional about what applies in your state.

TASKS

EXAMINE HOUSING

Housing is often a household's largest expense after income taxes. We never recommend a widow make major changes in her life in the year after the death of her husband. But, if you are looking at your income and expenses and moving is in your best interest, better to do it as soon as practical.

➡ If you are renting, talk to the landlord or property manager. While you can't break a lease early, if it's a larger apartment complex with different size apartments, maybe they'd be willing to let you move to a smaller unit.

➡ Family is often a critical component of our support network, and people often choose to live near family for that reason. If you have young children, you might move closer to your parents. If you're older, you might move closer to your children. Before you put the house on the market or sign that lease, make sure you have a conversation with your family. Take your time.

➡ A big house is a big pain in the neck for most widows. A big house is more expensive in every way - property taxes, maintenance costs, utilities, landscaping, etc... Before you downsize to that two bedroom condo, take your time to consider where you want to live. There's no point buying a condo in the town where you and your husband lived only to realize a year later that you want to move closer to a family member.

➡ Beware the illusion of control. It is human nature to feel anxious and stressed when many things are happening that are beyond your control. Being widowed is certainly a situation where you have little control. As humans, our fight or flight response to stress often results in feeling like we need to act. Selling the house or moving soon after your husband's death is a common way widows try to exert control over their circumstances. Resist the temptation until you've gathered all the information you need and have spoken with family, friends and a trusted advisor.

Not Just A Widow Guidebook

STAGE 5 CONTENTS

"Let the memories fill your mind and warm your heart. Let happiness lead you forward."

INTRODUCTION

T ime has passed. As the months turned into years, you have continued to evolve. We define Stage 5 as roughly two years after your husband's passing and beyond. You're amazed by how far you've come, but you still experience grief and sadness. It's natural. When we told you at the beginning of your journey that you couldn't imagine where you'll be at this point, were we right? When we told you not to do anything permanent in the first year, do you understand why?

The journey isn't completely over, but hopefully you can look to the future and feel good about what you see. Take time to reflect on what it took to get here and note all the surprises you've experienced along the way.

Welcome to the new YOU sister!

PATTY'S SISTERLY ADVICE

I f you're like many other widows, you've seen a few changes over the last two years. The changes aren't always visible from the outside, though.

I know I felt like a different person two years after Basil died, but I wouldn't say my journey was complete until after seven years when I moved from Maryland to Alabama.

In those seven years, I sold a house, lived in two apartments and moved over a thousand miles to be close to family. I built up my business and started Not Just A Widow, LLC with Doug. We created this guidebook.

I celebrated birthdays and anniversaries without Basil. I've had good days and bad. I've felt Basil's presence in my life and know he is keeping an eye on me.

I've lost touch with some old friends. I've met some incredibly strong women who I love dearly. I've opened myself up to meeting someone new, but no man has been what I needed.

I've learned to be independent and trust my own judgement. I'm more confident than I was before Basil died. I'm taking steps to make sure I have a healthy future - physically and financially.

I am a widow. But I'm not just a widow. I'm so much more. The widow in me is a significant part, but it doesn't define who I am and what I do. I've moved past widowhood. You will too.

Over time you will likely have people in your life who never met your husband, never knew you as his wife. They only know the new you. It can be nice to interact with these people without the reminder of your husband. Let yourself be happy.

Live life to its fullest. Life's too short not to enjoy. But you know that...

RETIREMENT PLAN - There are a number of different types of retirement plans employers offer employees. The most common are 401(k)s and 403(b)s. There are also pension plans, SEPs, and SIMPLEs. Federal employees have access to the Thrift Savings Plan (TSP).

PRENUPTIAL AGREEMENT - A contract entered into by a couple prior to marriage or civil union that enables them to select and control many of the legal rights they acquire when marrying and what happens to assets when their marriage ends by death or divorce.

CAT-FISHING - To lure someone in a relationship by means of a fictional online persona. Cat-fishing is a bizarre phenomenon that rose out of social media.

LEGAL AGREEMENT - Is a written document that will identify the parties' roles and responsibilities under the agreement. This means that if either party fails to perform his or her duties under the agreement, he is in breach of contract.

IDENTITY THEFT - The fraudulent acquisition and use of a person's private identifying information, usually for financial gain.

RETIREMENT PLAN - There are a number of different types of retirement plans employers offer employees. The most common are 401(k)s and 403(b)s. There are also pension plans, SEPs, and SIMPLEs. Federal employees have access to the Thrift Savings Plan (TSP).

PENSION - A pension is monthly payments from a former employer. When the pension owner dies, the payments may stay the same, get reduced or stop altogether depending on the payout selected when the pension was started.

ANNUITY - An annuity is an insurance product. Annuities are very complex and there are many options available.

WILL - The legal document where a person names a Personal Representative, how their property should be distributed and, if there are minor children, who should be their guardian.

BENEFICIARY - The person or persons to whom property is to be distributed upon the owner's death. The property goes directly to the beneficiary(ies) and is not part of the probate estate.

POWER OF ATTORNEY - Also called a POA, it is a signed document that gives a person or persons legal authority to make legal and financial decisions on your behalf (but not healthcare related).

HEALTHCARE POA/HEALTHCARE DIRECTIVE - It is a signed document that gives a person or persons legal authority to make healthcare decisions if you are unable to provide instructions yourself due to your incapacity.

5 CHANGES YOU NEVER WOULD HAVE IMAGINED

➡ **BECOMING INDEPENDENT** A married couple, like most teams, utilize a division of labor. One spouse is primarily responsible for one set of tasks, the other spouse has their own. You makes decisions together (or at least the big ones). One of the changes you've experienced is that you're now responsible for it all. No doubt there are tasks you didn't enjoy or never needed to learn how to do because your husband did them. As an independent woman you are responsible for it all. You've had to learn some new skills and find some new people to help you get things done. But you did it.

➡ **FEELING LESS SECURE** One of the unspoken benefits of a married couple is the security that comes with knowing your spouse has your back. You face challenges together. If there is an accident, illness or unexpected event one person is dealing with, the other spouse can pick up the slack. Single people don't have a partner to rely on. You might have your children, but that's different. Widows often comment that they worry more about their future and unexpected events than they did before their husband died.

➡ **LONELINESS** Long-term couples enjoy an intimacy that widows miss early on. Obviously there is sex and sexual intimacy, but that's different from general intimacy couples enjoy by living in the same house, doing things together, sharing a bed, etc... Children, family and friends simply don't provide that deep intimacy that many humans crave. It's why we seek out our partners.

➡ **TRUST LESS** Because you are older and wiser, because of your new found independence, because of your heightened sense of insecurity, it is likely that you are less trusting than you were before your husband died. The irony is that your desire to protect yourself makes you guarded and therefore less likely to achieve that same level of intimacy you enjoyed with your husband.

➡ **FEAR OF GETTING SICK** As we get older, the fear of getting sick and not having a child or close family member near by can be overwhelming. As wonderful as nurses and doctors are at patching us up, it's not the same as having someone who knows you available just in case something unexpected happens. The support of family is why they tend to live close by and you may find you want the same sense of security family offers.

THOUGHTS ON DATING AND GETTING REMARRIED

It probably goes without saying that dating and relationships won't be the same. You're not the same person you were when you met your husband. You're older and wiser. Be open minded about what you might feel. It's ok to be disappointed you don't feel exactly the way you did with your husband, but don't prevent yourself from being happy. Don't let anyone's expectations about what is appropriate or acceptable prevent you from having a happy relationship with someone. That's for the two adults in the relationship to decide.

One challenge you may face is finding a mature man to have a relationship with. Statistically, women live longer, which means there are fewer and fewer men your age as you get older. In addition, widowers tend to get remarried at a higher rate than widows do. Many women choose to not remarry and you may not want to either.

If you are considering remarriage, have a frank discussion with your partner about his financial circumstances and whether you're putting yourself at risk by marrying. Most states have laws that prevent one spouse from dis-inheriting the other. You may want to keep assets and accounts separate. Consider the estate planning ramifications of remarrying - especially if you have children. Your children may not receive your property if you die before your new husband unless you take steps to ensure it. Talk to a financial planner and/or an estate attorney before tying the knot again.

THOUGHTS ON PLANNING FOR THE FUTURE

Your circumstances are unique to you - it goes without saying. So when it comes to giving advice about your future, we can't possibly give any specific advice. What we do know, from talking to many widows, is that it takes years for your new life to settle out. Maybe it's two years; maybe it's ten years. We think it's unrealistic to expect you to figure everything out inside of two years.

Given this, our advice is to be open minded about who you are, what you want to do and where you will be in the future. Don't paint yourself into a corner too early in this process. Don't do anything that can't easily be undone. For example:

➡ Don't remarry right away.

➡ If you move, rent - don't buy.

➡ Stay healthy.

➡ See a fee-only financial planner and make sure you understand your financial circumstances.

YOUR GRIEF JOURNAL

Experts agree that it can be therapeutic to write your thoughts and/or experiences down on paper. The process of writing is more important than what you actually write down. We have provided space below for you to express yourself however you see fit.

YOUR GRIEF JOURNAL

TASK OUTLINE

As the months become years and you approach the end of your transformation, there are a few final tasks to make sure you complete. They are important, but for most people they aren't the most time sensitive. They will also symbolize that you are ready to become the new you since your outlook will have changed.

✓ Update Your Legal Documents.

✓ Confirm & Update Your Beneficiaries.

✓ Keep Track of Income You Can Claim In The Future.

✓ Planning For The Future.

TASKS

UPDATE YOUR LEGAL DOCUMENTS

It's a good idea to update your estate planning documents every few years regardless, but after your husband's death it's especially important to make sure everything is in good order and to make any necessary changes.

- ➡ **Will -** Attorneys usually name spouses as each other's personal representatives/executors. An alternate or two is often named as well. Talk to your attorney about removing your husband as personal representative and naming at least two trusted individuals for the job: one as first choice and one as back-up. If you had any specific bequests in your Will, you should make sure those are still in-line with your wishes.

- ➡ **Power of Attorney -** Married couples often give their spouses power-of-attorney in case they are incapacitated and can't make legal or financial decisions. This document should be updated. Remember that this power generally goes into effect as soon as you sign the document and continues until you revoke it in writing or you die.

- ➡ **Healthcare Directive -** Married couples often grant each other the ability to make health care decisions, access medical records and provide end of life instructions. Update this important document by naming a trusted family member or friend.

- ➡ **Trust Documents -** If you have a revocable trust (also called a living trust) or some other type of trust, you should talk to an attorney about updating the document. You may need to adjust the successor trustees as well as how, when and to whom the trust pays income and principal.

UPDATE BENEFICIARIES

Beneficiaries are the people (or charities) you name to receive some of your money or assets directly. Money or investments that are paid directly to a named beneficiary do not go through the Will (avoiding probate). Below are some of the places most people name beneficiaries. You should confirm who is currently named for each account and then update the beneficiary(ies) as necessary.

→ **Life insurance -** Your original insurance application will show if you named a beneficiary. Your current statement might list the beneficiary. If in doubt, call the insurance agent on the statement, call the insurance company's customer service number, or log into your account on the insurer's website to confirm. Likewise, if you have life insurance through your employer, confirm that policy's beneficiary.

→ **Retirement plans and IRAs -** Employer retirement plans usually list beneficiaries on their web sites. Traditional and Roth IRA custodians (i.e. Schwab, Fidelity, Vanguard) send a form every year called a Form 5498. It lists the current beneficiaries of the IRA. Alternatively, you can look online or call the custodian. Beneficiaries can be updated on the custodian's web site, or they can provide you a form to make updates. You simply complete it, sign it and send it back.

→ **Bank accounts -** The beneficiary of a bank account is called payable-on-death or POD. Sometimes they are listed on statements or can be confirmed on the bank's web site, but you might have to go to a branch and ask someone to confirm. A POD is not the same thing as a joint owner or signor. A person named as POD can't access the account or the money until you have died.

→ **Investment accounts -** Similar to the POD on bank accounts, brokerage and mutual fund accounts have a transfer-on-death designation (TOD) which allows the account owner to name a person or people who will receive the money upon the death of the account owner.

TASKS

KEEP TRACK OF FUTURE INCOME SOURCES

If you were widowed before you and your husband retired, there may be survivor benefits that don't get paid until you are older. It is imperative that you keep documents and information related to any benefit you are due.

→ **Social Security survivor benefits in retirement -** Widows are eligible to receive benefits on their husband's Social Security as early as age 60. Talk to Social Security six months before you turn 60 for more information and to confirm benefits. If your benefit, based on your own earnings, is higher, you can switch over to that amount any time between age 62 and 70.

→ **Pensions -** If your husband accrued a pension benefit from a former employer, they often provide a survivor benefit. Make sure you retain documentation about what the benefit is, when it starts and who to contact.

→ **Retirement plans -** If your husband has a balance in an old employer's retirement plan, you can access that money when you retire. There are income tax consequences and special rules to be aware of as a spouse. Consult the custodian of the plan and an independent fee-only financial advisor before you do anything with this money.

→ **IRAs -** If your husband has traditional or Roth IRAs, you can access that money when you retire. There are income tax consequences and special rules to be aware of as a spouse. Consult the IRA's custodian and an independent fee-only financial advisor before you do anything with this money.

PLANNING FOR THE FUTURE

When your life has settled down and you have had a chance to think about the future, it's time to do some long-term planning.

➡ If you are still working, how prepared are you for retirement? What will your income sources be in retirement? When should you start Social Security benefits or pensions? How will your savings and investments provide for you in retirement? Where will you live?

➡ If you're already retired, are you sure your income sources and savings will last? Most people need some sort of physical assistance as they age. Who will provide this assistance to you? Is there a family member or do you need to investigate a retirement or assisted living community?

An experienced financial planner can discuss options with you and help answer many of these questions. Avoid financial planners who sell investment or life insurance products since their advice is limited to and dependent on the products they sell. Don't hesitate to ask them how they get paid. There are plenty of financial planners who can help you for an hourly fee or a fixed fee without insisting that you buy something or that they take over management of your accounts. If you can't find one locally, many planners offer advice remotely or virtually.

Not Just A Widow Guidebook

Sister Stories To Inspire

"My mission in life is not merely to survive,
but to thrive; and to do so with some passion,
some compassion, some humor and some style."

- Maya Angelou

Ruth's Story

I was 48 years old when my husband died after a 14 month battle with pancreatic cancer. I was a nurse at a local hospital and mother of 2. My daughter was 20 and in her second year of college. My son was 18 and has severe Autism. I was lost and confused on how life would go on. My son needs 24 hr. care, and over my 30+ year career I worked nights so that my husband was at home with him while I worked and vise versa. My daughter was attending a private college that cost over $30,000 per year. We owed more on our house than what we originally paid due to refinancing and a second mortgage to pay for my son's needs. My mother died 10 months before my husband of breast cancer, and my dad was a very sick man (he's since passed also). My in-laws were both deceased (I cared for my mother-in-law in our home for 3.5 yrs until she died). I was on my own, scared and lost to say the least. With some good friends who guided me and two life insurance policies, I was able to survive. Health insurance was a major issue due to my son's disability, but again we made it through.

We are faithful in our home, and I prayed a lot. It has been seven years since this my husband died, and when I look back on how we got through the first two years, I can say anything is possible. Life insurance paid off house. My daughter's college gave us some help with reduced costs the first year after we lost my husband. I was able to pay off her student loans with the rest of the life insurance. Social Security disability benefits have helped me care for my son so I could retire. I can't say that it was always easy, but we did it. Life has gone on.

My daughter graduated from college with honors and is teaching 5th grade. She is engaged and bought a house close to me. My son graduated from high school with a certificate and was able to get help through the Developmental Disability Association. He is able to go into the community with hired help to do volunteer work. I am able to work in my garden (my therapy) or go for hikes with our dog as often as I want. Being a full time caretaker for an adult with a disability can be a challenge in itself, but I am doing it and I am able to also go out with friends at times.

To my widow sisters, I tell you to believe, to pray, and to ask for help (beg if you have to). Remember life will go on, and it does get easier. Do I miss my husband? Yes! Everyday I think of him, and our plans for our retirement. Is it easy? Not always, but I know that I can do pretty much anything after surviving such a trauma before I turned 50. God Bless!

Your Story

Are you interested in sharing your story with other widows? Not Just a Widow was founded on the idea that widows who have completed their transformation are the ones best able to help new widows. In future editions of this Guidebook, we intend to add more stories so new widows can read about the trials and successes of their widow sisters who came before them. We want to provide a diverse combination of stories. Contact us via our web site at **www.notjustawidow.com** and let's see how your story can inspire other women.

ACKNOWLEDGEMENTS

No project of this scope can be completed without the help, insight and encouragement of many people.

Patty and Doug would like to collectively thank Kim Zavrotny, Senior Funeral Director, of McComas Funeral Homes for always giving us her time and talent for this project. Kim has been a great resource and we appreciate her support.

Patty would like to thank

- The "WITs" (Women In Transition): Barbara, Karin and Ruth. Your love and support these past nine years have been incredible. Thanks for always being in my corner.

- My family for always being there and giving me advice on this project. Your love and support have assisted me in getting this book finished.

- My partner Doug R. for your honesty and support. This project has been a wonderful experience. That day in December at lunch seems like yesterday when you said to me, "thought about writing a book about your experience" and I said I already started it. Let's work together.

Doug would like to thank:

- My wife Patty R. for your love, support and insight as I started yet another "project", but one that you recognized early on could help so many other women in their time of need.

- My book partner Patty D. for your patience as we tried to get this guidebook "just right" and for your candidness as we talked about what widows experience and feel, but don't really talk about with non-widows. I've learned so much from you as we've travelled this crazy journey from that first meeting between you, Basil and I.

- Jeanne, Rita, Karline, Ashlee and the many other widowed clients who have given me the opportunity to help them with their personal finances and gain the experience and insight needed to be a valuable resource to other women.

- Diane Howard, dear friend and infamous Grief Girl who not only let me see the grief you experienced when you lost your beloved Doug, not only let me help you through your journey as you came to terms with your new reality, but also invited me to write a chapter on personal finances for widows for your own book. (*I'll Remember You; The Journey Back From Loss* written with Noreen Katz). This all began with you.

Not Just A Widow Guidebook

Not Just A Widow Guidebook

Not Just A Widow Guidebook

Made in the USA
Middletown, DE
12 May 2021